BEFORE YOU SAY "YES" AND "I DO"

'Til Death Do You Part

Understanding God's Mind

on

The Natural and Spiritual Union

Sonya Johnson Driver

BEFORE YOU SAY "YES AND "I DO"

Published in the United States of America

Copyright © 2019 by Sonya Johnson Driver.

All rights reserved. No part of this publication may be reproduced, stored in a retrieval system, or transmitted in any form or by any means, electronic, mechanical, photocopying, recording, scanning, or otherwise, without the prior permission of the publisher.

ISBN: 978-1-7341353-0-5

Empower Publishing

P. O. Box 1507

Cleveland, TX 77328

TABLE OF CONTENTS

Acknowledgments 9

Introduction 13

Chapter One: In the Beginning 17

Chapter Two: Created in His Image 23

Chapter Three: Creation Covenant 35

Chapter Four: ... Male and Female Created He Them 45

Chapter Five: Purity 61

Chapter Six: God Blessed Them...Be Fruitful and Multiply 89

Chapter Seven: Before You Say "Yes" and "I Do" 119

Prayer of Encouragement 128

Prayer of Salvation 129

Resources 131

ACKNOWLEDGMENTS

All praises to the Most High "Yah" God. Thank you for your love and patience with me Daddy God. It is because of your word this book was written and a reality. You called me out of my comfort zone and required this writing of me for your glory.

To my three beautiful daughters, Brittany, Crystal and Destiny, I am grateful for your love and support in whatever…WORK! WORK! WORK! WORK! WORK! WORK! (inside joke), community projects, Back to School drive, catering or whatever endeavor I decided to do, you all are always in the midst with me. Desi, thank you for nagging me to finish the book, we did it.

Mother, Brenda Molizone, you are an amazing mother. You have been my #1 cheerleader and support throughout my life. Thank you for your unconditional and unwavering love and care for me. I love you to the moon and beyond.

To my late father, William, I know you would be so proud. I can hear you say, "Neek, you and the Lord been busy. What do you have the Lord working on now?" LOL. Daddy, I love you and miss you so much.

Pastor Arthur Molizone, my stepfather, thank you for always availing yourself to the girls and me whenever and whatever the need might be.

A special thanks to a dynamic couple, my brother Eric and sister Elaine. You guys have undergirded my family through some critical issues. Thank you for your tireless love and support. Love you much!

In my journey, God placed people in my life to influence my life path. To my Kingwood First Baptist Church family, Daddy God used you to answer an unspoken prayer. You have been more than an employer to my family and me. Thank you for allowing the Father to use you to be a tremendous blessing to us. I am forever thankful and grateful for every act of kindness and love shown to us throughout the years.

To my Nigerian brother Uwa and sister Joy, you engrafted my family into yours and have been a tremendous blessing to us.

Mr. and Mrs. Darrell Hancock words can't express my thoughts towards you. It has been a joy working with the two of you over the years. Mr. Hancock, I will forever be grateful for your willingness to lend your expertise to assist me during a difficult transition in my life.

Thank you for seeing me as your sister in Christ. I love you both.

In His Love,

Sonya

I wrote "Before You Say, "Yes" and "I Do",
to help the reader to look beyond the fanfare
of the wedding day

,

Introduction

"Before You Say, "Yes" and "I Do" was written to illuminate the spiritual and natural covenant God instituted during creation. The chronological account of creation does not mention specifically of the natural or spiritual covenant; however, we will explore both covenants. What is the concept of the covenants? What was God's purpose and plan for the two covenants?

The book will explore God's mind concerning the two intertwined relationships; the natural union between man and woman, the spiritual union between God and mankind will be revealed through his word. As well as, understanding how the natural covenant mirrors our spiritual covenant with God.

For thy Maker is thine husband; the LORD of hosts is his name; and thy Redeemer the Holy One of Israel; The God of the whole earth shall he be called. Isaiah 54:5

The spiritual covenant is a two-fold component. The individual's spiritual union with God and the spiritual purpose of the "two becoming one" in the natural marital union. Honestly, the spiritual aspects of marriage may not be in the forefront of our minds before saying, "Yes". However, God's counsel should be considered whether the person of your choice is the person He would deem suitable for your destiny. Would your union fulfill his purpose and plan for your lives? Would it mirror the love and care God has for his Church? We tend to act according to our desires independent of God's counsel in the matters.

God foreknew each person born on the earth and he has a divine purpose and plan for each person as the following scripture confirms.

Jeremiah 1:5 "Before I formed thee in the belly, I knew thee; and thou camest forth out of the womb I sanctified thee, and ordained thee a prophet unto the nations."

With Jeremiah 1 verse 5 in mind, God knows the plan he has for your life, so before getting engaged to someone, it's essential for each individual to discover their purpose God has brought them forth to accomplish on the earth. Discovering your purpose will aid you in knowing if a prospective mate will be a suitable complement to your destiny, which is a very important factor indeed.

After going through my divorce from my husband of 26 years, I found myself doing an autopsy on my failed marriage. What were the contributing factors that ultimately dissolved my Christian marriage?

My mind went back to the night my then boyfriend asked me to marry him. We had been dating off and on for 3 years at the time. When he asked me, at first, I thought he was joking, but to my surprise he was serious. Prior to his proposal, I don't recall us discussing getting married, nonetheless, I said, "Yes". From the night of his proposal in October of 1986 to the day of our wedding in May of 1987, we never discussed our expectations for our marriage or what marriage meant to us individually. So, needless to say, we surely didn't think about the spiritual component of the marriage. In essence, after the proposal and during the engagement, we planned for the wedding day without giving thought to the marriage. Neither did we collectively seek God's counsel about us getting married, the "two becoming one", uniting in "Holy Matrimony" and how we would navigate the "becoming" of the marriage successfully.

I wrote "Before You Say, "Yes" and "I Do", to help the reader to look beyond the fanfare of the wedding day, instead understand God's mind and purpose for the natural marital union for his glory. And most importantly, understanding the spiritual union and covenant each person has with God and the eternal blessing (life) God vow to give us.

It's essential to discover your purpose for being before getting married.

CHAPTER ONE:
In The Beginning...

"In the beginning God created the heaven and the earth. And the earth was without form, and void; and darkness was upon the face of the deep. And the Spirit of God moved upon the face of the waters." Genesis 1:1-2

Every day we are beneficiaries of someone's creative concepts that have changed our way of life. Consider the evolution of technology, such as computers, telephones, the internet, and cars. There was a time none of these existed, however, someone was inspired out of necessity and/or creativity. To receive the full ultimate intended benefit from the creator's product, one would need to understand the concept of the device and the manufacturer's manual (guidelines and instructions) on the proper intended use of the product for the ultimate product operation.

Respectfully, for this book, to understand God's concept for his creation, we need to start at the beginning of his creation manual for our optimum life experiences, Genesis.

The first verse of Genesis solidifies God as the Creator of heaven, earth, and mankind. The chronological details of the first chapter of Genesis, we see God restore, create and set his concept for creation in order. He restored the earth to be inhabited once again. These details dispel the evolution theory, as believed by some in society as well.

I beheld the earth, and, lo, it was without form, and void; and the heavens, and they had no light. I beheld the mountains, and lo, they trembled, and all the hills moved lightly. I beheld, and, lo, there was no man, and all the birds of the heavens were fled. Jeremiah 4:23-25

For thus saith the Lord that created the heavens; God himself that formed the earth and made it; he hath established it, he created it not in vain, he formed it to be inhabited: I am the Lord, and there is none else. Isaiah 45:18

Vain- in Hebrew means *Tobu,* empty Strong's Hebrew – (Bible Hub)

Vain also means unproductive. God's creation concept from the beginning of his restoration of the earth was for it to be inhabited by mankind and animals. As we observe the order in which God worked to fill the earth, He chose to start life on earth with the animals. His decision to do so gives us a glimpse of his concept for creation.

And God said, Let the waters bring forth abundantly the moving creature that hath life, and fowl that may fly above the earth in the open firmament of heaven. Genesis 1:20

And God created great whales, and every living creature that moveth, which the waters brought forth abundantly, after their kind, and every winged fowl after his kind: and God saw that it was good. Genesis 1:21

And God blessed them, saying, Be fruitful, and multiply, and fill the waters in the seas, and let fowl multiply in the earth. Genesis 1:22

Blessed-highly favored, endowed, supplied, granted; characterized by happiness. [FreeDictionary.com]

In verse 22, the word *blessed* is an unexpected term in this text regarding the animals. The blessing is God's declaration of provision for the animals and a blessing for reproduction. God was endowing the animals the ability to carry out his command to reproduce after their kind. As we know, God is the creator of life and the only one that can cause something to reproduce of itself.

Throughout scripture it is evident, God operates on the basis of an agricultural concept. He desires fruitfulness. As a farmer work to cultivate a field to make ready to plant seeds, at the appointed time, he is expecting an abundant harvest for his labor. This is God's concept for his creation as well.

Hidden in the scripture of the blessing and command is the covenant. The covenant with the animals as God's creation shows the pattern of the symbolic nature of our covenant relationship with God, his love, care, provision and ultimately the blessing for us, his human creation. As the animals live out their purpose to replenish the earth as God commanded, God promise he will be their provision. Whatever God purpose, he will make provision for its' success. This idea is explained in Matthew 6.25-26 *"Therefore I say unto you, take no thought for your life, what ye shall eat, or what ye shall drink; nor yet for your body, what ye shall put on. Is not life more than meat, and the body than raiment: Behold the fowls of the air: for they sow not, neither do they reap, nor gather into barns; yet your heavenly Father feedeth them. Are ye not much better than they?"*

An example of the covenant between the animals and God is exemplified in the account of Noah and the ark. God told Noah to build an ark and to take his family and specific numbers of male and female animals to preserve mankind and the animals. Scripture text did not say Noah had to go out to find or corral the animals on the ark. At the appointed time, God led the animals to Noah to preserve them during the flood so his concept for creation could continue as he planned from the beginning. [Genesis 6:17-20.] This account proves God's creation plan has everything to do with heritage and establishing his plan for mankind on the earth. Initially, God filled the earth with fowls of the air, beast of the field, creeping things, and fish in the sea. He established day and night, with the sun to shine in the day and the moon and stars for the night. At the end of verse 25 of Genesis 1, it says, "...and God saw that it was good". Everything that he had created was good because it was operating as he had designed. However, in the next chapter we will see God was not finished with his plan to fill the earth. In all that he created, it was good, but not perfect or complete.

God is the creator of life and the only one that can cause something to reproduce of itself.

CHAPTER TWO:
Created in His Image

"And God said, Let us make man in our image, after our likeness: and let them have dominion over the fish of the sea, and over the fowls of the air, and over the cattle, and over all the earth, and over every creeping thing that creepeth upon the earth." **Genesis 1:26**

One day I walked into my local Walmart and saw an older man sitting to the left of the store entrance. As I proceeded to walk past the gentleman, he spoke to me and asked me about my family name. I answered him with a "Yes Sir, that's my family". He told me he saw the resemblance. This was not the first time this had happened to me; however, it amazes me every time.

Honestly, as an offspring of my parents, I should resemble or have characteristics like one or both of them either in statue or character.

When a baby is born, the first thing that is observed about the baby, after it's gender, is which parent the baby resembles. It is a normal human propensity to determine the likeness in the physical attributes of the baby and parents. Procreating is a blessing and maternal or paternal pride to create a small human being in your likeness. For mankind to be made in the image and likeness of God, our Heavenly Father, it is a loving, glorious, powerful, and weighty blessing. It is the spiritual connection we have with him. Journeying through our everyday life, we are to display this spiritual connection by showing him love and giving him glory by living to honor him and obeying his word.

In the scripture text Genesis 1:26, "Let us", introduces The Father, The Son, and The Holy Spirit in this part of the text. We are to understand that even though God was used in a singular form until now, God denotes this unity.

In the beginning was the Word, and the Word was with God, and the Word was God. St. John 1:1

The same was in the beginning with God. St. John 1:2

All things were made by him; and without him was not anything made. St. John 1:3

"Let us make man in our image, after our likeness:" gives us insight into who we are. It separates us from all the other living creatures God made. This is a reality that I think we don't give much weight to its importance in our existence. For this reason, we have an influx of Life Coaches and Strategy Coaches in Christendom today? Their job is to help their client see themselves as God has empowered them. To understand the power and ability they possess inside of themselves. I believe it is this truth the enemy uses against God's children to hinder them from fulfilling God's plan and purpose for their lives. Going through life, we sometimes forget the endowment we have being a child of God. Being given dominion, power, and authority in the earth and how we are to display it in our life is important to grasp. God only referred to the human creation being made in his image. What words come to mind when you think about God's image or who he is? In the image of God, the Creator, Ruler, King, Holy One and the Almighty One. What an awesome awareness with boundless benefits and blessings to be a child of God.

Image – Heb. Tselum- resemblance.

Image-a likeness or imitation of a person or thing; a person strikingly like another person; a vivid representation of or to create a representation of. [Webster Dictionary]

Likeness- Heb. Demuwth- resemblance shape, model; and refers to outward form. [Webster Dictionary]

When we think of the image and likeness of God, we must think about holiness, love, compassion, righteousness, kindness, intellect, creativity, power, and authority (dominion).

...and let them have dominion over the fish of the sea, and over the fowl of the air, and over the cattle, and over all the earth, and every creeping thing that creepeth upon the earth. Genesis 1:26

Dominion – 1. Domain; 2. Supreme authority; 3. Sovereignty 4. Self-governing Nation of the commonwealth Webster New Dictionary

Domain – a territory over which dominion is exercised; 2. Complete and absolute Ownership of land; 3. A sphere of knowledge, influence or activity. Webster's New Dictionary

Commonwealth- 1. Is a traditional English term for a political community founded for the common good; 2. The noun commonwealth means public welfare, general good or advantage. 3. The body of people politically organized into a state. Webster New Dictionary

Sovereignty - supremacy in rule or power, the power to govern without external control. Webster New Dictionary

Domain and Dominion - our domain (territory) to exercise our God-given dominion is our homes, community and ultimately the world. Our King has already decreed our way of living in our domain in his word. It is in his word, he has declared for us to have dominion (supreme authority), self-governing by the word of God our King. We are to be an influence in the world, displaying a God-likeness life.

Take heed to thyself, lest thou make a covenant with the inhabitants of the land whither thou goest, lest it be for a snare in the midst of thee: Exodus 34:12

But ye shall destroy their altars, break their images, and cut down their groves: Exodus 34:13

For thou shalt worship no other god: for the Lord, whose name is Jealous, is a jealous God: Exodus 34:14

Lest thou make a covenant with the inhabitants of the land, and they go a whoring after their gods, and do sacrifice unto

their gods, and one call thee, and thou eat of his sacrifices; Exodus 34:15

And thou take of their daughters unto thy sons, and their daughters go a whoring after their gods, and make thy sons go a whoring after their gods. Exodus 34:16

God used his relationship (covenant) with the children of Israel for our example in relating to him. God was their King, he promised them provision, a land for them to dwell and a place to worship him. They were to live by his word, however, as they sojourned, they observed the culture of the people in the land and desired to live like them. [Exodus 34:12] The people of the surrounding area the children of Israel encountered had natural kings and idol gods. Their lifestyle was totally against God's law and his desire for his chosen people. [Exodus 20:4-6] Consequently, the children of Israel disobeyed and suffered for their rejection and disobedience to God.

We, as his chosen people, are to resolve and relinquish any and all gods that we have placed supreme in our lives instead of the one and only wise God, who requires supreme authority in our lives through his word.

To understand the meaning of the word commonwealth, it helps us better understand how it relates to God's plan.

Commonwealth is comprised of the root word "common", meaning "belonging to all, and "wealth" meaning happiness or riches. Commonwealth is a noun that also means a politically organized body of people under a government. [Vocabulary.com]

When we look at the meaning "belonging to all", "a body of people under a government", "riches and happiness", we see God's kingdom covenant. God's plan was displayed in Adam and Eve in the garden before they sinned against him. Everything they needed naturally to live was provided. Spiritually, they were in the presences of God. God's love and blessings are for all of mankind. If we will allow his laws and statues govern our lives, blessed and happy will our lives be with God.

Sphere of Influence- a person's, country's, organization's etc. sphere of influence is the area where they have power to change things. [Idoceonline.com]

Sphere of Knowledge- unified body or collection of knowledge; (facts, information, awareness or familiarity gained by experience of a fact)., regarding a specific subject, interest or otherwise real of expertise possessed by an individual. [YourDictionary.com]

Sphere of Influence and Knowledge – as followers of God, we are to know and exhibit the lifestyle God has called us to live, to be an influence in our domain. We are to be the examples, the leaders and not followers of the culture of this world. This is why mankind was created; relationship and influence in the earth.

And be not conformed to this world: but be ye transformed by the renewing of your mind that ye may prove what is good, and acceptable and perfect will of God. Romans 12:2

Being made in his image and likeness makes us kings and rulers as he is the King of kings. If we are kings, the earth is our domain to rule as God has instructed. The earth is, in essence, our "kingdom" or king-domain. The activities or culture of the world should represent God's culture (his will) exemplified through our lives as his offspring. Romans 12:2 tells us to renew our mind-change our mind from a worldly cultural mindset, to prove what is good, acceptable and what is the perfect will of God's lifestyle for his kingdom. A sacrificial lifestyle unto God to display love, concern and care for all God's people.

God standeth in the congregation of the mighty; he judgeth among the gods. Psalms 82:1

I have said, Ye are gods; and all of you are children of the Most High. Psalms 82:6

For the Lord is a great God, and a great King above all gods. Psalms 95:3

Thine, O Lord, is the greatness, and the power, and the glory, and the victory, and the majesty: for all that is in the heaven and in the earth is thine; thine is the kingdom, O Lord, and thou art exalted as head above all. Both riches and honour come of thee, and thou reignest over all; and in thine hand is power and might; and in thine hand it is to make great, and to give strength unto all. I Chronicles 29:11-12

The Lord is good to all: and his tender mercies are over all his works. All thy works shall praise thee, O Lord; and thy saints shall bless thee. They shall speak of the glory of thy kingdom, and talk of thy power; To make known to the sons of men his mighty acts, and the glorious majesty of his kingdom. Thy kingdom is an everlasting kingdom, and thy dominion endureth throughout all generations. Psalms 145:9-13

God's plan for mankind is to build His "kingdom" culture on earth through us. One of my favorite ministers is the late Dr. Myles Munroe, he taught extensively about the Kingdom and the Kingdom culture. He referenced in a message from St. Matthew 6:9.

After this manner therefore pray ye:

Our Father- (the one we are created in his image and likeness)

Which art in heaven- (your dwelling place) Hallowed be thy name – (Holy Sanctified) Thy kingdom come – (thy order)

Thy will be done – (your purpose and plan)

On earth, as it is in heaven – (make manifest your will, culture, plans and purpose on earth as it has been established in heaven).

For thine is the kingdom – (you are King)

And the power and glory, forever Amen – (forever your Kingdom will stand...Amen "it is so") St. Matthew 6:9-13

Verily I say unto you, Whatsoever ye shall bind on earth shall be bound in heaven, and whatsoever ye shall loose on earth shall be loosed in heaven. St. Matthew 18:18

As sons and daughters of the King, it is imperative for us to intimately know God. Understanding our relationship with Him as our Father, the endowment of power and dominion he has entrusted us to possess in the earth. When a King makes a decree, it is done, it stands sure, no one can change it or come against it. We are to use the power of our Daddy God's word to fight against the attacks of the enemy in our faith, home, finances, health, churches, community and in the world.

It is in our relationship with our heavenly Father that we have true joy, peace, and victory.

In our relationship with God, we have to die to ourselves

CHAPTER THREE:
The Covenant

"And the Lord God formed man of the dust of the ground, and breathed into his nostrils the breath of life; and man became a living soul." Genesis 2:7

And the Lord God planted a garden eastward in Eden; and there he put the man whom he had formed. Genesis 2:8

And out of the ground made the Lord God to grow every tree that is pleasant to the sight, and good for food; the tree of life also in the midst of the garden, and the tree of know- ledge of good and evil. Genesis 2:9

The characteristic God attributed to mankind being made in his image and likeness was <u>dominion</u>. In Genesis 1:26, he said, "…Let us make man in our image after our likeness: <u>and let them have dominion…</u>" It was his desire to share his power and ability with mankind. Hence, with power comes responsibility, responsibility comes accountability, accountability equal covenant.

Covenant -*noun* – an agreement usually formal between two or more persons to do or not do something specified. Verb - to promise by covenant; pledge; an agreement between God and his people, in which God makes promises to his people and, usually, requires certain conduct from them. Dictionary.com

For thy Maker is thine husband; the Lord of hosts is his name; and thy Redeemer the Holy One of Israel; The God of the whole earth shall he be called. Isaiah 54:5

This scripture text tells us that our Maker, the Maker of mankind is our husband. God is our Maker and Husband. As our husband, we receive his image and likeness or in other words, his name. He assumes complete responsibility for our care and well-being spiritually and naturally. When a woman marries a man, she takes his image and likeness, she takes his name. In most cases, the woman drops her father's last name and take her husband's last name to signify their oneness and covenant. The significance of having a father's last name signifies his covering of his daughter and her as his responsibility for her provision, care, and well-being spiritually and naturally. So, when a man desires a wife, he is in essence, declaring to her Heavenly Father, as well as her earthly father, his desire to be the responsible man for her natural and spiritual care as emphasized in Ephesian 5. Likewise, with our spiritual covenant with God, we are to bear his name, image, and likeness through our upright living. We separate from our old name (character) to our new covenant name, God-like character.

As the husband of mankind, God prepared everything Adam needed in the Garden of Eden because he was in covenant with him. The covenant is not only for natural provision and care, but it is also, spiritual provision and care. The natural marital covenant is symbolic of the spiritual marital covenant with God.

Husband, love your wives, even as Christ also loved the church, and gave himself for it; Ephesians 5:25

That he might sanctify and cleanse it with the washing of water by the word, Ephesians 5:26

That he might present it to himself a glorious church, not having spot, or wrinkle, or any such thing; but that it should be holy and without blemish. Ephesians 5:27

So, when you think about the dynamics and expectations of a natural marital union, compare your ideology to the spiritual union with God. This passage of scripture in Ephesians mirrors our spiritual relationship with Christ and the husband-and-wife natural relationship. The elements required in the two relationships are sacrificial love, purity or sanctification by the word, and holiness. These elements produce God's desire. A glorious union together.

In a parent/child relationship, there is an unspoken covenant with the child or children in effect in the household. For provisions such as food, shelter, clothes and other wants and needs, the parent requires obedience, love, honor, and respect. Additionally, the things that are provided must be taken care of or there will be consequences and repercussions for the infractions of established household rules. LOL…old days child rearing.

Likewise, God's covenant with mankind, he loves us, provides for us, blesses us and he desires love from us and wants us to be obedient to his word. The heart of the creation covenant with man is "LOVE" and RELATIONSHIP". Everything God did was for his love for mankind and his desire to be in an intimate relationship with us. He gives us commands and instructions, so we know what is expected of us to stay in fellowship with him and ultimately not suffer separation from him. Therefore, God will, as a Father, correct us so that we can continue in fellowship with him. It is not his desire to be estranged from us, however, we must LOVE him with our whole heart, mind, soul and body.

And the Lord said unto Moses, Write thou these words: for after the tenor of these words I have made a covenant with thee and with Israel. Exodus 34:27

And he was there with the Lord forty days and forty nights; he did neither eat bread, nor drink water. And he wrote upon the tables the words of the covenant, the ten commandments. Exodus 34:28

And now, Israel, what doth the Lord thy God require of thee, but to fear the Lord thy God, to walk in all his ways, and to love him, and to serve the Lord thy God, with all thy heart and with all thy soul, To keep the commandments of the Lord, and his statutes, which I command thee this day for thy good? Deuteronomy 10:12-13

Know therefore that the Lord thy God, he is God, the faithful God, which keepeth covenant and mercy with them that love him and keep his commandments to a thousand generations; And repayeth them that hate him to their face, to destroy them:

he will not be slack to him that hateth him, he will repay him to his face. Deuteronomy 7:9-10

Although the scripture text in Genesis chapters1 and 2 does not literally note a formal agreement with God and Adam, however, Adam was given power and instructions by God, in essence, equates to covenant. Adam was accountable to God for the care of the garden. The covenant between God and Adam was a conditional covenant. Covenants are binding pledges with remedies if pledges are not fulfilled. Adam was to obey the instructions set forth in having dominion, in keeping the garden and obeying the rule of which trees were good for his use for food. God's instructions were very simple and doable, nothing that would cause Adam lack or hardship. Realistically, Adam was living his best life; he was in the presence of God walking through the garden without a care in the world.

And the Lord God took the man, and put him into the garden of Eden to dress it and to keep it. Genesis 2:15

And the Lord God commanded the man, saying, Of every tree of the garden thou mayest freely eat: Genesis 2:16

But of the tree of the knowledge of good and evil, thou shalt not eat of it: for in the day that thou eatest thereof thou shalt surely die. Genesis 2:17

In the next chapter, Genesis 3, we will see the significance of Adam's instructions and how it's imperative the "male" man knows God to righteously and effectively led his family in the ways of God. It is always safety in God's word and instructions to us.

Three time in the year all thy males shall appear before the Lord God. Exodus 23:17

During Adam's alone time, I believe God was allowing Adam time for self-discovery and time to display the likeness of God, his creator. Adam was walking in his authority and dominion, given the responsibility of keeping the garden as well as naming the animals. Most importantly, this time was also used for God and Adam to develop an intimate relationship. So it is with single individuals, during singlehood, it's a great opportunity to get to know God personally and intimately. Allowing God to show you his love for you and who you are in him. His purpose and plan for your life, as well as allow him to reveal to you issues in your life that need to be resolved, such as, immoral behavior, additions, unrealistic expectations of relationships, past hurts and baggage from previous relationships. Cultivating self-love, self-discovery and discipline are important facets to develop during singlehood as well.

One need to be spiritually and mentally whole for the success of their destiny and the success of a relationship. Sidenote, ladies and gentlemen, it's not a man or a woman's physique, talent, car, house, bank account or any material thing that qualifies a person an acceptable or suitable helper/mate for marriage. The physical material things are subject to change, however, their obedience and allegiance to God, knowledge of God, God-like character and wholeness can withstand the test of time.

Allow the scriptures to govern our lives according to the mind of God. Not according to what we see displayed in society, the belief and actions we know are contrary to the word. As a believer and follower of Christ, God's word is the only gauge we use to decide the acceptable way of living. Not only should we use the written word as our gauge for our natural and spiritual life, it is also to our advantage to seek him in prayer daily for guidance in making decisions. We declare God is all-knowing, however, we neglect consulting him for insight in our career choice, place of employment, residence, major purchases or decisions and last but not least our spouse. Seeking him for his wisdom of the future is prudent and wise counsel to minimize pitfalls, unnecessary stress and struggles.

"I will instruct you and teach you in the way which you should go; I will guide thee with mine eye." Psalms 32:8

He desires to be Lord of our lives, which means, we allow him to govern and instruct our lives for his glory. Not as a taskmaster, rather, a loving Heavenly Father that knows our future and what is best for us individually and as the family of God.

But ye are a chosen generation, a royal priesthood, an holy nation, a peculiar people; that ye should shew forth the praises of him who hath called you out of darkness into his marvelous light: I Peter 2:9

When we are tempted to be persuaded to the culture of the world, we must remind ourselves we are to be a light, a peculiar people. We are made in the likeness of God and our behavior should represent the character of God. I know it might seem living our life totally committed to God and his word is an impossibility in today's culture, nonetheless, it is what is expected by God. Dominate the culture to reflect the character of God through the influence of the children of God, those in covenant with him.

As I stated earlier, my objective is to explore the word to reveal the mind of God concerning his covenant with us, truth and not falsehood. Many teach the laws and commands are done away and we are under grace. This ideology has some believing they can commit sin/spiritual adultery and still be in covenant with God. To express your love to God, keep his commandments and refuse to bring shame to his name. To bring shame to God's name (his character) is to sin against his word. To rebel and disregard his word or instructions is rebellion against him, your way and not his way. Profaning his image by unholy behavior.

Profane-treat (something sacred) with irreverence or disrespect. Synonym: Desecrate, defile, pollute [Merriam-Webster.com]

Love not the world, neither the things that are in the world. If any man love the world, the love of the Father is not in him. 1 John 2:15

For all that is in the world, the lust of the flesh, and the lust of the eyes, and the pride of life, is not of the Father, but is of the world. 1 John 2:16

And the world passeth away, and the lust thereof: but he that doeth the will of God abideth forever. I John 2:17

CHAPTER FOUR:
...*Male and Female Created He Them*

"So God created man in his own image, in the image of God created he him; male and female created he them."

Genesis 1:27

God is so awesome. I love the wording of the end of Genesis 1:27, "male and female" created he "them". The fact God created the male human being Adam alone, however, the text says, "created he them", a plural pronoun. This wording magnifies God's omniscience and omnipotence. Scripture does not give us the amount of time between the creation of Adam and Eve. We know God foreknew Eve before he even formed Adam, however, his order symbolizes the "oneness" of the male and female human beings. God declared from the beginning that they would make the man in their image and likeness...created he <u>them.</u> Eve was already apart of Adam from the beginning and apart of God's ultimate plan.

Omniscience – having infinite awareness, understanding,

and insight. Webster New Dictionary of the English Language New Edition

Many of us have heard preachers preach about God giving Adam a job first before giving him the responsibility of a wife.

In Genesis 2:15, it does support this ideology.

And the Lord God took the man, and put him into the garden of Eden to dress it and keep it. Genesis 2:15

It was customary during Old Testament time, for a man to give a dowry to the parents of the woman he wanted to be his wife. The dowry was a sign to the parents that the man was able to take the responsibility to care for the woman instead of her father. Not only did he have to give the dowry, but he also had to go to prepare a place for her to live before she was given to him. This custom was the reason Jacob offered to work 7 years for Rachel's father to allow her to be his wife. The bible said

Jacob loved Rachel and the 7 years seemed but a few days. That was some real LOVE...LOL.

The unfortunate fact in society today, the standard of the man asking the father for the daughter's hand in marriage and demonstrating his ability to take care of her has been diminished. Factors that have contributed to this demise is fatherless homes, the breakdown of the family unit. The fathers are not in the home to teach their sons proper protocol or cover their daughters until marriage. Abandonment of God's way creates chaos, dysfunction, and brokenness in any given situation.

As I stated before, we were created to dominate the culture by God-likeness (God's way). So, of course, the enemy's goal is to cause us "mankind" to abort God's purpose and plan for our lives. As you look at the culture of today, it does not exhibit God's kingdom culture. God's kingdom is a theocracy and not a democracy.

Theocracy-government in which God is recognized as the supreme ruling authority, giving divine guidance to human intermediaries that manage the day-to-day human affairs of government. Wikipedia

Only the King can establish a way of life in his commonwealth. God started his kingdom first with the union between male and female human beings. Unfortunately, today's culture is reflecting its' opposition to God's design for the male and female covenant in these manifested thought processes.

-having a boyfriend or girlfriend with martial benefits is permissible

-marriage is not necessary

-marriage does not have to be between a male and female; same-sex is okay

-premarital sex is permitted

-having children out of wedlock is okay

-having a sexual partner outside of your marriage is permissible

-divorce and remarry multiple times until you find the one is okay…everybody is doing it

-marital commitment is not necessary…living together is acceptable…" Common-law",

"Cohabitation", "Shacking" and "Booed up"

In the first chapter of Genesis, the text says, "He blessed the animals, saying, "be fruitful and multiply". This revealed God's ultimate plan for creation...procreation. He knew beforehand the male human being would need a female human being just like the animals to fulfill his creation plan.

And the Lord God said, It is not good that the man should be alone; I will make him an help meet for him. Genesis 2:18

Adam was able to dress and keep the garden as charged by God alone, however, God could not charge him to be fruitful and multiply to replenish the earth without a suitable "help meet".

And Adam gave names to all cattle, and to the fowl of the air, and to every beast of the field; but for Adam there was not found an help meet for him. Genesis 2:20

Help meet-a helper as his counterpart. biblestudytools.com

Counter-something that is the opposite.

Counterpart-one of the two parts that fit, completely or complement one another. Dictionary.com

And the Lord God caused a deep sleep to fall upon Adam, and he slept: and he took one of his ribs and closed up the flesh instead thereof; And the rib, which the Lord God had taken

from man, made he a woman, and brought her unto the man. **Genesis 2:21-23**

Adam needed a "counterpart", a match, the opposite of himself, a womb human. Adam was capable of giving his seed, but he needed a human being with a womb to receive his seed to procreate. The woman God created for Adam had the ability to receive his seed and produce a being in their likeness. God's answer to Adam's "need" (requirement necessary to function and fulfill) was already placed in him from the beginning. However, she was not revealed to him until he had become who God had created him to be, a husbandman. Unfortunately, these days, the enemy has caused some men to abandon God's assignment for them to be husbands.

Husbandman-the master of a family; a farmer; a cultivator or tiller of the ground. [Webster's Revised Unabridged Dictionary.com]

Until men realize who they are and God's purpose for them, they will not fully understand their need for the female (woman) in regard to fulfilling their purpose in life. Dr. Tony Evans said in a meeting I attended, "if a man doesn't realize the value and gifts in his wife, he will never realize his full potential". We need men to embrace their purpose in the kingdom, being a husbandman. Embracing and mastering the responsibility of being the husband, priest, provider and protector of the family. A man's ability to produce an offspring does not make him a man or husbandman. The same is true for a woman, her ability to receive seed does not make her a suitable helper to a husband. Her willingness to submit to the leadership of her husband and prayerfully supporting him as he righteously guides the home is paramount. If both individuals understand the purpose and design of the institution of marriage, as well as the roles of both individuals in the relationship, the natural marital union will produce God's ultimate plan in the earth, righteous heritage. Another sidenote, God's desire is a righteous heritage, however, He gives each person a free will to choose the life one rather live. Righteousness unto God through Christ and the working of the Holy Spirit or defiance.

Spiritually, our helper, the Holy Spirit is our "need" (requirement necessary to function and fulfill) to produce God-likeness in our life. The opposition to our fruitfulness is spiritual barrenness and abortion. If we unite with a church body (a building) and engage in church activities, but no regards to repentance or no desire to change according to the word, we will be barren in the church building. A new life, a holy life can only be birth out by living according to the word, not church activities. When we hear God's word (his truth) in relating to him in love, holiness and righteousness, if we reject (abort) the truth, again, we cannot produce a holy life. As long as we reject the word of God and consequently the indwelling of his spirit, we will forever be spiritually barren. We can't produce God-likeness with an unlike God-life. Obeying the word of God will produce a new spiritual life with God. The spiritual life, our union with God produces is eternal life with him for us individually, as well as anyone our lifestyle influences a relationship with God.

For Adam to fulfill God's charge to him to "be fruitful and multiply" it cost him apart of himself. Adam had to sacrifice one of his ribs to form his God-given suitable helper.

Sacrifice means to accept the loss or destruction of for an end, cause or ideal. To offer up or kill as a sacrifice. [Webster New Dictionary of the English Language]

In a marriage relationship, the man has to accept the loss of selfishness and self-centeredness when he is given a wife. He has to be willing to live sacrificially for the welfare of his wife and family. By no means am I insinuating that only the husband is required to sacrifice selfishness or self-centeredness; both the husband and wife have to be willing to deny their self-centered thoughts, ways, and desires. Being selfish in a relationship will never produce oneness or cohesion. It will certainly cause division and death in the marriage.

And Adam said, This is now bone of my bones, and flesh of my flesh; she shall be called Woman, because she was taken out of Man. Genesis 2:23

So ought men to love their wives as their own bodies. He that loveth his wife loveth himself. Ephesian 5:28

God's design, "Holy Matrimony".

Holy – worthy of absolute devotion; sacred; having a divine quality – [Webster New Dictionary of the English Language New Edition]

Matrimony- marriage. [Webster New Dictionary of the English Language]

Marriage- the state of being united to another as a contractual relationship according to law and custom. [Webster New Dictionary of the English Language]

Therefore shall a man leave his father and his mother, and shall cleave unto his wife: and they shall be one flesh. Genesis 2:24

At the appointed time, God brought Eve forth out of Adam and united them to carry out his plan for their existence in the earth. So, it is with us, we must remind ourselves that God has the master plan for our existence, and we must be willing to do his will.

Before I formed thee in the belly, I knew thee; and before thou camest forth out of the womb I sanctified thee, and I ordained thee a prophet unto nations. Jeremiah 1:5

You might be wondering how does this scripture coincide with marriage? Individually, God knew us before our parents conceived us. He knows the purpose and assignments he has for us to accomplish during our lifetime, so our life is about more than self-gratification or just seeking to get married. So, in other words, to be married to someone should not be the ultimate goal for our lives. As a child of God, we should be like Jesus, fulfill our Father's will for our life first. Jesus came to sacrifice his life for the redemption of mankind back to His Father. He came to accomplish his purpose and assignment.

For I came down from heaven, not to do mine own will, but the will of him that sent me. St. John 6:38

God is the creator of mankind. He created each of us for his purpose and glory. There is no one born that God did not have a purpose for their life. In your singleness, you should seek him for his plan and vision for your life before considering marriage. Discovering your purpose and personal gifts will give you insight into your ability to be a suitable helper to a prospective mate. Your individual gift(s) need to enhance your prospective mate's purpose. So, when the two of you come together, the vision for your covenant will not be a divided vision. Your union will be cohesive and will display to the world its likeness to God's relationship with his church. So, entering into "Holy Matrimony" is a serious matter to God, it is his design and his purpose for the natural and spiritual union with the male and female.

Husbands, love your wives, even as Christ also loved the church, and gave himself for it. Ephesians 5:25

For no man ever yet hated his own flesh; but nourisheth and cherisheth it, even as the Lord the church. Ephesians 5:29

For we are members of his body, of his flesh, and of his bones. Ephesians 5:30

For this cause shall a man leave his father and mother, and shall be joined unto his wife, and they two shall be one flesh. Ephesians 5:31

This is a great mystery: but I speak concerning Christ and the church. Ephesians 5:32

Nevertheless, let every one of you in particular so love his wife even as himself; and the wife see that she reverences her husband. Ephesians 5:33

The natural marriage, the man and woman are to be committed to one another. The relationship "holy" and "sacred" (set apart) from any other relationship with individuals outside of the marriage. Your relationship with your spouse is to be on a higher level than any other including your parents. The charge to couples to "love" and "cleave" to one another to become one in vision and purpose. Be the lover of your spouse's soul and life to spiritually nurture in obedience to the word of God. Not to cause your mate to sin against God before or during the marriage. Anything you love or is of great importance to you, you purposely take extra care. Marriage was designed to enrich one's life. It is a gift. It's to be enjoyed all the days of your lives together.

We know when "divorce" becomes a topic in a marriage, "division" has become prominent than cleaving. Divorce is the result of a divided vision within the marriage union. This is why the willingness to sacrifice self-centeredness and selfishness completely for the marriage to thrive. Marriage is a daily dying to self-process for the marriage to live. The two becoming one.

In our relationship with God, we have to die to ourselves (our image and will) as well, to seek God's will for our lives and fulfill his plan. Seek his wisdom and insight. In the church world, we tend to pursue the images we have in our heads for our lives instead of seeking God's will for us. In essence, we become our own god, ruling authority of our life. We worship (give devotion) to the images and desires we have for ourselves independent of God's plan. Sometimes we exalt ourselves to positions God didn't call us to operate in. Titles become gods, and our purpose gets lost. One thing to consider, God's plan for us is far greater than anything we can imagine or produce on our own. The creature will never be greater or more powerful than the Creator. Lucifer is a great example of this fact. Lucifer had a prominent position in heaven with God and was said to be beautiful, decked with an array of precious stones, however, he was not satisfied with the life he had in God's kingdom. He wanted to be higher than God.

Thou wast perfect in thy ways from the day that thou wast created, till iniquity was found in thee. Ezekiel 28:15

By the multitude of thy merchandise they have filled the midst of thee with violence, and thou hast sinned: therefore I will cast thee as profane out of the mountain of God: and I will destroy thee. O covering cherub, from the midst of the stones of fire. Ezekiel 28:16

Thine heart was lifted up because of thy beauty, thou hast corrupted thy wisdom by reason of thy brightness: I will cast thee to the ground, I will lay thee before kings, that they may behold thee. Ezekiel 28:17

Lucifer's sin against God was rebellion. The purpose God created for him was not sufficient to him. He created and pursued the "image" in his mind for himself, independent of God's purpose and position. This is the tactic Satan used on Adam and Eve and he is still using it today because it is effective in separating God's people from Him. It is the image of God that we are to keep in the forefront of our mind (forehead) to obey and not the image of the beast to rebel and disobey. I admonish you not to take on the mindset of the beast of this world system, self-sufficiency and rebellion, the end result will be eternal separation from God. God's word is true and the final authority.

And the third angel followed them, saying with a loud voice, If any man worship the beast and his image, and receive his mark in his forehead, or in his hand, Revelation 14:9

The same shall drink of the wine of the wrath of God, which is poured out without mixture into the cup of his indignation; and he shall be tormented with fire and brimstone in the presence of the holy angels, and in the presence of the Lamb: Revelation 14:10

And the smoke of their torment ascendeth up for ever and ever: and they have no rest day nor night, who worship the beast and his image, and whosoever receiveth the mark of his name. Revelation 14:11

Truthfully, we are either in covenant with God our Creator or in covenant with his adversary, the beast, the antichrist.

Food for thought: When we do things our way, we in actuality have elevated ourselves to "god" in our life.

Idolatry- the worship of a physical object as a god. [Webster's New Dictionary of the English Language]

An idol is an object of passionate devotion. An image worshipped as a god. A false god. [Webster's New Dictionary of the English Language]

An idolater is a worshipper of idols – [Webster's New Dictionary of the English Language] god – a being or object believed to have supernatural attributes and powers and to require worship. [Webster New Dictionary of the English Language]

God – the creator and ruler of the universe and source of all moral authority; the supreme being. Syn. the Lord, the

Almighty, the Creator, the Maker –[Webster New Dictionary of the English Language]

Enter ye in at the strait gate: for wide is the gate, and broad is the way, that leadeth to destruction, and many there be which go in thereat: Because strait is the gate, and narrow is the way, which leadeth unto life, and there are few who find it. Matthew 7:13-14

In hope of eternal life, which God, that cannot lie, promised before the world began; Titus 1:2

CHAPTER FIVE:

"And they were both naked, the man and his wife, and were not ashamed." Genesis 2:25

Purity – freedom for evil or sin; innocence; chastity; freedom for adulterating matter; freedom from corrupting elements. Synonym: Cleanliness, Virtue, integrity, honesty, innocence [Collinsdictionary.com]

Innocence-fact of being innocent; lack of guile or corruption; purity; [Oxford Dictionaries]

"Man's state in innocence" is the heading above the text Genesis 2:25 in my bible. The best analogy to describe the state of innocence of Adam and Eve would be two opposite sex newborn babies sharing a crib. Babies are the epitome of innocence. The basis of their consciousness of their existence consists of nursing, sleeping, crying, and excrement. Babies aren't aware of gender, nakedness, the need for clothes, manners, right or wrong behavior, or anything pertinent to their survival aside from the aforementioned four natural functions. Unlike newborn babies, Adam and Eve were fully grown, capable to utilize God's provision for their natural needs, and they were not created with a sinful nature. Purity at the purest form, freedom from evil or sin, nothing to inhibit their fellowship with God. Unfortunately, we know the fellowship was compromised in the next chapter.

Now the serpent was more subtle than any beast of the field which the Lord God had made, And he said unto the woman, Yea, hath God said, Ye shall not eat of every tree of the garden? Genesis 3:1

And the woman said unto the serpent, We may eat of the fruit of the trees of the garden: Genesis 3:2

But of the fruit of the tree which is in the midst of the garden, God hath said, Ye shall not eat of it, neither shall ye touch it, lest ye die. Genesis 3:3

And the serpent said unto the woman, Ye shall not surely die: Genesis 3:4

For God doth know that in the day ye eat thereof, then your eyes shall be opened, and ye shall be as gods, knowing good and evil. Genesis 3:5

Chapter 3 of Genesis details the consequences of Adam and Eve breaking their covenant and union with God. As I read this passage of scripture, two thoughts came to mind. First, curiosity of the length of time expired between the end of chapter 2, the sweet fellowship with God, and the beginning of chapter 3, the beginning of the demise of the sweet fellowship. Secondly, why was Eve entertaining a dialogue with an animal, a creature of the field, a lower being than she and her husband? Realistically, how can the serpent interpret the instructions God gave to her husband? Actually, her response to his commentary should have been a quick dismissal back to his dwelling place. Instead, she allowed the serpent to give his interpretation of the instructions God had given to her husband. The serpent, in essence, told Eve that God lied to them, "Ye shall not surely die". He led her to believe it was no big deal to eat of the tree. When did the creature become greater than the creator? In verse 5, we see Satan's most effective tactic against mankind then and even today, he appeals to the lust of the human being to be the ruler or god of their own existence. Adam and Eve had a good existence in the garden. They had sweet communion with God and everything they needed naturally in the garden. However, in verse 6, Adam failed to exercise his God-given headship, authority, and dominion over his wife and the creatures in the garden. Adam and Eve's disobedience to God caused them to become impure, it revealed awareness of their nakedness and shame seeing the need to cover themselves. Their disobedience did not dissolve their marital covenant; however, it did dissolve their ability to live forever in pure fellowship with God and one another. Ultimately, they could no longer fellowship with God as before their disobedience.

And when the woman saw that the tree was good for food and that it was pleasant to the eyes, and a tree to be desired to make one wise, she took of the fruit thereof and did eat, and gave also unto her husband with her; and he did eat. Genesis 3:6

And the eyes of them both were opened, and they knew that they were naked; and they sewed fig leaves together, and made themselves aprons. Genesis 3:7

Ladies, I know I may have struck a nerve with some of you by stating, "Adam didn't exercise his God-given headship, authority, and dominion over his wife". Yes, the man is the leader in the home. The husband should seek God for wisdom to lead the family. He is the first partaker in any duty or responsibility necessary for the well-being and safety of his family. Men, as a husband, you cannot be a male chauvinist or a narcissist in your role as the leader of the home. The husband as the leader of the home does not mean the woman is to be treated as a doormat, a slave, non-essential or a lower being than himself. If a husband considers himself superior to his wife, he does not understand the role of the wife to his existence and purpose in the earth. Technically, it is a fact that both spouses are to be subject to one another, discuss things concerning the household and family matters together. Ephesians 5:21-24. However, the final authority rests with the husband in regard to guiding the home. If being submissive is a problem for you, I would advise you to wait to get married and seek premarital counseling to address this issue. The prerequisite for reverent submission to the husband is his submission to God. It is not blind submission.

Ladies, if you earn more money than your mate, it does not make you the leader or head of the relationship or household.

You are to be a suitable helper. Being an independent whole woman in waiting, once you are found by your mate, you will need to wisely adjust your independence for the health and success of the relationship and household.

In verse 6 of Genesis 3, Eve stepped into the mindset that she, the creature, was greater than her Creator. She knew what was good for her regardless of what God commanded. I wanted to bring this point out because our culture is plagued by this mindset, thinking God's statues aren't necessary to completely obey. We think we know what is best for ourselves than God. Having this mindset is very dangerous for our hope in fellowship with God and eternal life with him.

In the Dake's Annotated Bible it gives commentary for Genesis 3:7: Knew before mentally but know by experience. They lost "God" consciousness and gained "self" consciousness. They lost the power to do good and gained the power to do evil. Thus, instead of becoming like God they became unlike Him in that He has the power to do only good. It is morally impossible for Him to sin. Adam lost that glorious sinlessness and innocence looking countenance comparable to that of Elohim.

Their disobedience changed them from who God created them to be...like him - holy. They became unholy and unrighteous. God's original way of life for mankind and their union with God totally changed forever by this one act of disobedience. They broke the spiritual covenant and fellowship with God by leaning on their own interpretation of what God commanded. They stepped outside of God's provision for their well-being. Disobeying God's word, which is our covenant with God, separates us and causes death in our relationship and fellowship with Him. God is holy and righteous, therefore, to fellowship with him he requires us to be as he is, holy and righteous. Spiritually pure to be joined in a covenant with God.

Be ye not unequally yoked together with unbelievers: for what fellowship hath righteousness with unrighteousness: and what communion hath light with darkness? 2 Corinthians 6:14

And what agreement hath the temple of God with idols? For we are the temple of the living God; as God hath said, I will dwell in them, and walk in them; and I will be their God, and they shall be my people. 2 Corinthians 6:16

Wherefore come out from among them, and be ye separate, saith the Lord, and touch not the unclean thing: and I will receive you, 2 Corinthians 6:17

And will be a Father unto you, and ye shall be my sons and daughters, saith the Lord Almighty. 2 Corinthians 6:18

Adam's natural and spiritual life was tied to his oneness and fellowship with God in the garden. God was the husbandman to Adam, as Adam was to Eve. God provided everything for Adam to be Eve's husband. The same is true for men being a husbandman when they take a wife. Proverbs 18:22 says, Whoso findeth a wife findeth a good thing, and obtaineth favour of the Lord. Men, favour with God is far better than any favour from a man. What an awesome privilege God bestows on men that takes one of his daughters to wife.

Favour -approval, support, or liking for someone or something; an act of kindness beyond what is due or usual. [Oxforddictionaries.com]

The term husband is not used until Genesis 3:6 when Eve gave the fruit to her "husband".

Husband – a male partner in a marriage; master of a house- Webster New Dictionary of the English Language New Edition

House-band – connecting and keeping together the whole family. Easton Bible Dictionary

The Easton Bible dictionary house-band definition exposes the reason why our homes and communities are in disarray. The connectors and keepers of the family are absent from the home or nonexistent.

As a husband, the man's role is to be a priest, provider, and protector. According to scripture, the priests were responsible to teach God's laws and ways. They were to seek God for guidance and instructions on leading the people for their well-being and union with God. The priest's role was a sacrificial role as well. The priests had to be holy/pure (Godly character). Likewise, as the priest of the family, the husband is to be the example of Godly character, the first partaker in knowing God, worshipping him, communicating with him, and learning his ways to teach and lead his family according to God's statutes and standards.

The following scripture text reference God's standards for the priests:

They shall be holy unto their God, and not profane the name of their God; for the offerings of the Lord made by fire, and the bread of their God, they do offer; therefore, they shall be holy. Leviticus 21:6

Profane – to treat (something sacred) with abuse, irreverence, or contempt; not holy because unconsecrated, impure or defiled. [Merriam-Webster]

Thou shalt sanctify him therefore; for he offereth the bread of thy God; he shall be holy unto thee; for I the Lord, which sanctify you, am holy. Leviticus 21:8

In the New Testament, Jesus used the word "bread" as an analogy of himself in St. John 6:33-35.

For the bread of God is he which cometh down from heaven and giveth life unto the world. St. John 6:33

Then said they unto him, Lord, evermore give us this bread. St. John 6:34

And Jesus said unto them, I am the bread of life: he that cometh to me shall never hunger; and he that believeth on me shall never thirst. St. John 6:35

As the priest, it is the duty of the husbandman, the father, to know God and lead his family according to God's commands. Throughout scripture, the patriarch of the family would receive guidance from God for the safety and wellbeing of his family. Noah is a good example of knowing God for the benefit of his family. Genesis 6:8-9. The scripture text says, "...Noah walked with God." Noah exemplifies the importance of hearing the voice of God to save his family alone from God's judgment on the world during the flood. In the New Testament, Joseph, the husband of Mary, was instructed to take his family to safety to flee the massacre decreed by King Herod.

Today, we see the devastation of our communities and the world due to the absence of the priests in the home. Men not being in a relationship with God to teach and lead their families, as well as being a role model in the community.

As a provider, God provided everything Adam and Eve needed to live in the garden before Eve was presented to Adam. Adam was charged to "dress" and "keep" the garden. He was given the means to provide for Eve. In the book of Ruth, Boaz instructed his workers to leave Ruth some good portions and to allow her to glean in his fields before he became her kinsman redeemer and husband.

As the protector, Adam was charged to "keep" the garden. The garden was the dwelling place for Adam and his wife, Eve. Unfortunately, Adam failed in this area when they listened to the serpent twist God's instruction. When Eve offered the fruit to Adam, Adam knew he had been instructed not to eat of that particular tree. He was responsible to take authority and obey God's instruction even though his wife ate of the fruit. He ultimately was the one that personally knew what God commanded. Their eyes (consciousness) were not opened until

Adam ate of the fruit. Adam and Eve's sin (eating the fruit) against God was rebellion against his word, not in an immoral or sexual nature. Satan tempted them with the one thing they were instructed not to partake. The tactic of the enemy is the same for us today, his playbook is the same, the temptation with self-sufficiency. His ultimate goal is to break our fellowship with God by causing us to sin against his word. Sin is to miss the "mark" (path) that God has set for our life. Not doing the things we know God desires from us.

But every man is tempted, when he is drawn away of his own lust, enticed. James 1:14

Then when lust hath conceived, it bringeth forth sin; and sin, when it is finished, bringeth forth death (separation from God). James 1:15

In my study for this chapter on purity, I found in the Old Testament, God set specific rules for the priest concerning their way of life. The priests were required to be holy and consecrated unto God. Therefore, the priest's perspective wife had to be a virgin (pure and undefiled).

They shall not take a wife that is a whore, or profane; neither shall they take a woman put away from her husband: for he is holy unto his God. Leviticus 21:7

And he shall take a wife in her virginity. Leviticus 21:13

A widow, or a divorced woman, or profane, or an harlot, these shall he not take: but he shall take a virgin of his own people to wife. Leviticus 21:14

In the Old Testament time, there were very strict laws concerning a woman's virginity. A woman was to be a virgin when she was taken to wife. Purity as relating to virginity (abstinence of sexual intercourse before marriage) was a very important custom for the Israelites. The woman could be put to death if she was found to be defiled (not a virgin). The husband would go before the elders of the city to plead his case against his wife being defiled. Seeking the elders to render a judgment or bill of divorcement in his favour, releasing him from the marriage. Parents of the young woman would collect and keep the bed cloths after the marriage was consummated for this cause. If the husband brings an accusation of defilement against their daughter, the parents would bring the bed cloths to present as proof of her virginity. Read Deuteronomy 22:13-29

But if this thing be true, and the tokens of virginity be not found for the damsel: Deuteronomy 22:20

Then they shall bring out the damsel to the door of her father's house, and the men of her city shall stone her with

stones that she die: because she hath wrought folly in Israel, to play the whore in her father's house: so shalt thou put evil away from among you. Deuteronomy 22:21

The message to us in this passage of scripture lets us know we cannot be defiled, being the bride of Christ. Christ is our High Priest so his bride has to be pure in heart and deeds.

In today's culture, surprisingly, purity is a hot topic and a great debate among Christian singles. Most men and women don't consider being a virgin before marriage as an expectation of God. Nor, do they consider it as a standard requirement for today. God is holy and his institution of marriage is a holy and sacred covenant, therefore, we must honor his word and design for the martial covenant.

I heard a story of an exercise a teacher conducted with her class to cause her students to think about sex in a different light. She asked each of her students to let her have their cell phone; each student understanding the value and love for their phone replied with the same answer, "NO". The teacher asked, "Why do you easily give your bodies to consensual sex"? She wanted them to understand protecting and saving their bodies is more important than protecting their cell phones. The same resounding "NO" to giving their cell phones away, should be the same resounding "NO" to anyone wanting to engage in premarital sex.

Let's think about the scriptural account of Mary, the virgin, mother of Jesus in Luke 1:26 - 30.

And in the sixth month the angel Gabriel was sent from God unto a city of Galilee, named Nazareth, Luke 1:26

To a virgin espoused to a man whose name was Joseph, of the house of David; and the virgin's name was Mary. Luke 1:27

And the angel came in unto her, and said, Hail, thou that art highly favoured, the Lord is with thee: blessed art thou among women. Luke 1:28

And when she saw him, she was troubled at his saying, and cast in her mind what manner of salutation this should be. Luke 1:29

And the angel said unto her, Fear not, Mary: for thou hast found favour with God. Luke 1:30

What an honor for Mary to receive from Gabriel, the angel, the messenger of God. The salutation such as this, "Hail, thou art highly favored, the Lord is with thee: blessed art thou among women". Why was Mary highly favored? It would be safe to say Mary was not like all the other women in her area in some way.

She had to have some qualities that set her apart for God to take notice and favor her to carry his Son, Jesus the Christ, the Word. For the task at hand, Mary's virginity was an important aspect and a requirement for her ability to carry Jesus, our High Priest. We do know she lived her life unto God due to the following statement in Luke 1:28, "the Lord is with thee".

Also, according to Leviticus 21, the priest could only marry a virgin of "his people". This requirement was necessary for the priest because of the standards of the priest's office. His wife would need to know and understand the laws of God for his chosen people, the Israelites. Being an Israelite herself, she would have been taught the laws and customs of God from her parents, as we are to do for our children today.

Therefore, Mary had to be pure (a virgin) vessel for her to carry the "Son of God", our "High Priest" and the "Word". Purity is essential in relating to God no matter what the culture or standards of the world.

And the daughter of any priest, if she profane herself by playing the whore, she profaneth her father: she shall be burnt with fire. Leviticus 21:9

Beloved, the scripture references I have noted may seem hard to digest. My objective is to help us understand the mind of God.

Being made aware of the truth is "love" towards you. No, we are not stoning and burning women to death for not being virgins, however, this shows you the weight of the matter in God's eyes. Men, God is just; you are not excused from being sexually pure as well. God hates sin and requires it to be removed out of our lives. Spiritual purity is essential, God will not and cannot join himself or dwell in sin and disobedience.

Reflecting on Leviticus 21:9, we are not to profane our Heavenly Father's name by playing a harlot, spiritually defiled by sin, before people of our influence. Defilement causes eternal fiery separation from God, our Father. Both men and women alike, if we profess ourselves sons and daughters of God, believers, Christians, women of God, men of God, or any office of the 5- fold ministry of God, it is imperative we truly love God and keep his commandments/statues. We cannot live double lives. To receive the promise of the covenant, eternal life with him, we must remain in spiritual covenant with him. We are to sanctify ourselves to be pure unto him. Likewise, if it be God's will to bless us that we have a natural marriage, we are to love our spouse, be pure and sanctified unto them, as unto God.

Know ye not that ye are the temple of God, and that the Spirit of God dwelleth in you? 1 Corinthians 3:16

If any man defile the temple of God, him shall God destroy; for the temple of God is holy, which temple ye are. 1 Corinthians 3:17

Let a man so account of us, as of the ministers of Christ, and stewards of the mysteries of God. 1 Corinthians 4:1

Moreover, it is required in stewards, that a man be found faithful. 1 Corinthians 4:2

…Now the body is not for fornication, but for the Lord; and the Lord for the body. 1 Corinthians 6:13b

Know ye not that your bodies are the members of Christ? shall I then take the members of Christ, and make them the members of an harlot? God forbid. 1 Corinthians 6:15

What? Know ye not that he which is joined to an harlot is one body? For two, saith he, shall be one flesh. 1 Corinthians 6:16

But he that is joined unto the Lord is one spirit. 1 Corinthians 6:17

We are all sinners before salvation, we were born with the sinful nature in our being. It is when we are made aware of our need for salvation/reconciliation with our "Holy" God, our Father; repentance is required for salvation and change must take place. Jesus was sent to earth to be the way to salvation and reconciliation to God. It is the righteousness and holiness of Jesus Christ's life that we have the opportunity and ability to be holy and righteous.

I indeed baptize you with water unto repentance: but he that cometh after me is mightier than I, whose shoes I am not worthy to bear: he shall baptize you with the Holy Ghost, and with fire: St. Matthew 3:11

Wherefore gird up the loins of your mind, be sober, and hope to the end for the grace that is to be brought unto you at the revelation of Jesus Christ; 1 Peter 1:13

As obedient children, not fashioning yourselves according to the former lusts in your ignorance: 1 Peter 1:14

But as he which hath called you is holy, so be ye holy in all manner of conversation; 1 Peter 1:15

Because it is written, Be ye holy; for I am holy, 1 Peter 1:16

Believing in Christ and his crucifixion is believing that after repenting, dying to yourself, receiving the spirit of Christ and the power it brings, you are empowered to live holy before God. The embodiment and power of the Holy Spirit enables you to make righteous choices. The power given to us is the power to walk righteously in our everyday walk by the spirit that lives on the inside of us after repentance. This statement might produce disbelief in some; however, we must submit ourselves to the mind and word of God.

To illuminate a symbolic comparison of the natural union covenant and the spiritual union covenant, we know the children of Israel were required to offer animal sacrifices and other "sweet savour" offerings to God for a sin offering or one of several offerings God required for specific purposes. Offerings are detailed in the book of Leviticus.

And he bought the bullock for the sin offering: and Aaron and his sons laid their hands upon the head of the bullock for the sin offering. Leviticus 8:14

And he slew it; and Moses took the blood, and put it upon the horns of the altar round about with his finger, and purified the altar, and poured the blood at the bottom of the altar, and sanctified it, to make reconciliation upon it. Leviticus 8:15

But as many as received him, to them gave the power to become sons of God, even to them that believe on his name: St. John 1:12

Which were born, not of blood, nor of the will of the flesh, nor of the will of man, but of God. St. John 1:13

God instructed Moses to have Aaron and his sons, which were the high priest for the children of Israel; to kill a bullock for a sin offering unto God. This duty could only be carried out by the high priest. The blood of the animal was placed on the altar in the tabernacle as symbolic to placing it before God. It was also symbolic of being reconciled unto God in a spiritual union, being one spirit with him. Now, instead of the animal sacrifices as offerings to unite us with God, God sent his Son to be the ultimate sacrifice to unite mankind back with God. When God created the creation, the man was the only creature he made in his image and likeness, so an animal sacrifice (the value) was not equal to man. So, God sent Jesus to be transformed into the form of man for a blood sacrifice, "sweet savour" an acceptable offering, to reconcile mankind back to him. For this reason, Jesus is called our High Priest and the Lamb of God.

The next day John seeth Jesus coming unto him, and saith, Behold the Lamb of God, which taketh away the sin of the world, St. John 1:29

In the natural marital union, the man and the woman, after their wedding (vow) ceremony, consummate the marriage by coming together as one through sexual intercourse. God in his omniscience created a membrane in the female genital called the hymen. When the couple consummates their marriage through sexual intercourse, the hymen breaks and blood is released from the woman onto her husband (her priest). Symbolic of a blood covenant between the two and their union witnessed before God. For this reason, marriage is not to be entered into without knowledge, understanding and wise counsel.

Marriage is honorable in all and the bed undefiled, but whoremongers and adulterers God will judge. Hebrews 13:4

To honor God in our natural union, we have to love and be committed to God's holy institution of marriage. Deny fleshly desires to give yourself sexually to someone other than the person you vowed and made a covenant with before God. Sex is, in essence, a spiritual act in God's eyes. God designed it for a holy purpose. We have allowed the enemy to entice us through the culture of the world to not obey what God has established for his glory and purpose. We have made the lust for sex the foundation of our relationships and not God's order and purpose of the sex act. It is believed in today's society that a couple must have premarital sex to determine sexual compatibility before committing to marry. This belief is not biblical at all, it is a fleshly and a carnal mindset which ultimately is not pleasing to God. Premarital sex and sex outside of your marriage is not 'holy' and is totally unlike God. Experiencing premarital sex with multiple partners can cause issues and problems within the marriage due to unspoken expectations of your spouse based on previous sexual partners. If sex is experienced for the first time by both spouses, both will be able to learn how to sexually please the other and will not have any experiences to compare. Sexually pleasing yourself by masturbation and with pornography can and will be a problem for the marriage as well. God's design for sex is the right way and for our best interest.

Adultery is voluntary sexual intercourse between two unmarried persons or two people not married to each other. [Dictionary.com]

Whoremonger means someone who consorts with whores. [Dictionary.com]

Fornication is voluntary sexual intercourse between persons not married to each other, which would include adultery (voluntary sexual intercourses with a partner other than your lawful spouse) [got questions.org]

In the natural covenant, both spouses are expected to be faithful and not give any cause to jealousy. If outside attention or sexual involvement is revealed, there will be hurt, jealousy and mistrust that will cause division in the marriage. As I noted earlier, division causes divorce in relationships. You should keep your focus on your spouse and the union you share with God in order to keep out evil influences from penetrating your marriage.

As with the natural covenant, certain behaviors can cause a spouse to be jealousy, so it is with God. He created us for a relationship with him and he does not want us to yield our body to sin, any evil forces or wrong mindsets. He is jealous for us as well. He sees us as his bride, His heritage.

For thou shalt worship no other god: for the Lord, whose name is Jealous, is a jealous God: Exodus 34: 14.

Satan, the evil one, is the enemy to our union with God. It is his desire to try to get us to rebel against God's standards and behave in a way that is not pleasing to God and his desired relationship with us. We are not our own to do as we will.

Now when I passed by thee, and looked upon thee, behold, thy time was the time of love; and I spread my skirt over thee, and covered thy nakedness: yea, I sware unto thee, and entered into a covenant with thee, saith the Lord God, and thou becamest mine. Ezekiel 16:8

Then washed I thee with water; yea, I thoroughly washed away thy blood from thee, and I anointed thee with oil. Ezekiel 16:9

I clothed thee also with broidered work, and shod thee with badgers' skin, and I girded thee about with fine linen, and I covered thee with silk. Ezekiel 16:10

I decked thee also with ornaments, and I put bracelets upon thy hands, and a chain on thy neck. Ezekiel 16:11

And I put a jewel on thy forehead, and earrings in thine ears, and a beautiful crown upon thine head. Ezekiel 16:12

Thus wast thou decked with gold and silver; and thy raiment was of fine linen, and silk, and broidered work; thou didst eat fine flour, and honey, and oil: and thy wast exceeding beautiful, and thou didst prosper into a kingdom. Ezekiel 16:13

And thy renown went forth among the heathen for thy beauty: for it was perfect through my comeliness, which I had put upon thee, saith the Lord God. Ezekiel 16:14

But thou didst trust in thine own beauty, and playedst the harlot because of thy renown, and pouredst out thy fornications on every one that passed by; his it was. Ezekiel 16:15

The Hebrew word translated "**fornication**" in the Old Testament was also in the context of idolatry, also called spiritual whoredom. [Got Questions.org]

This passage of scripture shows the spiritual covenant with God and the children of Israel. We are not called the children of Israel; nonetheless, we are his children; this passage can give us some insight into God's heart towards us and the spiritual covenant he has with us. When we allow sin to have a place in our life, we have broken the covenant with God. He has loved us, redeemed us, taken care of us, providing us with our wants and needs, however, we choose to play a spiritual harlot. Committing spiritual adultery is denying the truth of God's word, giving ourselves to false beliefs, doctrines and ungodly behavior.

In closing this chapter on purity, this scripture text explains God's love and care for the children of Israel, yet they chose to break their covenant with him. Everything he provided for them was not good enough for them to reciprocate his love by being faithful to him. Believe it or not, Christendom is in this very state today, as this scripture details. Some Christians today want the blessings of God, but not give themselves totally to him and to his standards. They reject real love (truth) and embrace falsehood to their detriment.

Love not the world, neither the things that are in the world. If any man love the world, the love of the Father is not in him. 1 John 2:15

For all that is in the world, the lust of the flesh, and the lust of the eyes, and the pride of life, is not of the Father, but is of the world. 1 John 2:16

And the world passeth away, and the lust thereof: but he that doeth the will of God abideth for ever. 1 John 2:17

The fact that people are choosing not to marry, but want the covenant benefit of sex, God's gift of sexual intimacy for the natural marital union has been extremely perverted today. Perverted not only by sex without marriage, extramarital affairs, homosexuality, lesbianism, pornography, and prostitution; the sex slave trade has reached epidemic proportions all over the world. The lust for money and sex has created an insatiable appetite for sex with young girls and boys. In the sex trafficking industry, young people are being abducted every day and forced to become a sex slave for the rest of their lives, if not miraculously rescued. They are taken from their families and life as they knew it and put into a world of sex slavery. Their innocence is stripped away and introduced to sex in a perverted and defiled way. They may never experience marriage and sex as a gift as God intended. I pray for an end to this horrible industry and deliverance for the victims involved.

God's design is always the best way to live life.

But now being made free from sin, and become servants to God, ye have your fruit unto holiness, and the end everlasting life. Romans 6:22

For the wages of sin is death; but the gift of God is eternal life through Jesus Christ our Lord. Romans 6:23

CHAPTER SIX:
God Blessed Them... Be Fruitful and Multiply

"And God blessed them, and God said unto them, Be fruitful, and multiply, and replenish the earth, and subdue it: and have dominion over the fish of the sea, and over the fowl of the air, and over every living thing that moveth upon the earth."
Genesis 1:28

When you hear the word "blessed", do you equate it's meaning to money, cars, houses or some type of material possession? The Christendom culture of today has conditioned many to equate this meaning mindset when we hear this term. The term "blessed" meant something vastly different during bible days. The term "blessed" was first used in Genesis 1:22 when God blessed the animals to procreate after their kind to fill their inhabitants. So, the term "blessed" used in the first chapter of

Genesis, has nothing to do with our interpretation of blessed in today's culture. A "blessed" status was comparative to how many children you birth, not solely on your possessions. God's blessing to mankind in Genesis 1:28 was a blessing to procreate a being in his image and likeness. Heritage is God's plan for his creation. With this in mind, we can understand why Hannah desperately cried out to God for a "man" child.

Lo, children are an heritage of the Lord: and the fruit of the womb is his reward. Psalms 127:3

As arrows are in the hand of a mighty man; so are children of the youth. Psalms 127:4

Happy is the man that hath his quiver full of them: they shall not be ashamed, but they shall speak with the enemies in the gate. Psalms 127:5

God blessed Adam and Eve with sons, Cain, Abel, Seth and other sons and daughters not named in scripture. They were not only blessed with children; they had a "blessed" beyond measure life before their fall. God blessed them to be in perfect fellowship with him. What a blessing that is…one on one with God. Everything needed to live was provided for them. As the expression goes, "they were living their best life". Good news, God has blessed each of us with life here on earth and the opportunity to live as Adam and Eve did before their fall. We are invited to accept his invitation to fellowship with him; enjoy an abundant life on earth and eternal life with him. As an appendage of the abundant life, God has blessed us with the gift of the natural marital covenant to enjoy as he instituted with the first natural marital covenant between Adam and Eve. The ability to unite with someone to do life with, someone to build with, procreate with and to fully enjoy life together until death do you part. This is God's desire for mankind. However, today, we aren't seeing many marriages nor are we seeing longevity in marriages. We are experiencing very high divorce rates even among Christian marriages. Christian marriages should be immune to the divorce statistic. Honestly, it should not be named among the body of Christ. However, ignorance (lack of knowledge) is one of the reasons this statistic is a fact of life today. The primary focus of couples after becoming engaged tend to be only on the wedding day. The wedding day is one day, and it does not encompass the marriage. The wedding day is the sign or witness of the "vow" to be united to one another. The logistics of the "vow", the two shall "become" one, 'til death do you part, is obscured by the wedding day fanfare. We have become desensitized about what the wedding day represents. We get deluged in choosing the wedding dress, choosing the colors for the wedding, who to have in the wedding party, wedding location, and other wedding day details. More times than not, there is no dialogue concerning expectations each person has about the marriage. Conversations about conflict resolution, finances, expectations concerning having children, parenting styles or individual thoughts on divorce aren't discussed in detail, if at all. So truthfully, the vision for the marriage, God's purpose for the marriage and why the couple chooses to get married is not really discussed in most cases. Premarital counseling is not considered necessary by many couples. Counseling should be a requirement to qualify for obtaining a license to marry. This might seem radical; however, I think couples would be better equipped for married life and the possibility of divorce and broken families would be minimized.

Men and women marry for different reasons. Some marry to alleviate loneliness, wanting the feeling of being loved by someone, limitless sex, financial benefits, live-in housekeeper, kids, and family. You might be able to add to this list with reasons you are getting married or why you desire to get married.

Honestly, most of us aren't thinking, "Oh, I need to get married to fulfill my destiny and purpose in the earth". LOL.

When I said, "yes" to my boyfriend's proposal at the age of 18, I did think about the prophetic word spoken in regard to him being called to the ministry, as a Preacher. I did consider the type of wife I would need to be to support him in his calling, a suitable helper to him. I didn't want to be a hindrance to God's plan for his life. However, I realized at the time, I didn't think about the possibility of God having a specific purpose for my life to complement his calling. I neglected to discover my purpose or calling before saying, "yes" to his proposal. Nonetheless, I was consumed with the fanfare of the wedding day and not so much the marriage afterward as often is the case during the engagement phase.

After the wedding, at some point in most marriages, (the blessing) the God-given desire to procreate becomes the focus of the couple. God's creation concept for the marital covenant naturally being fulfilled. Why we desire to have children, I'm not sure. I conclude it's because God made us by nature the desire to procreate, display our likeness of Him. God's heritage, the divine concept for mankind. He desires healthy whole family relationships with him as the cornerstone.

For the duration of this chapter, we will focus on the bountiful blessing God promised to Abraham and Sarah regarding their seed, Isaac.

And Abram and Nahor took them wives the name of Abram's wife was Sarai; and the name of Nahor's wife, Milcah, the daughter of Haran, the father of Milcah, and the father of Iscah. Genesis 11:29

But Sarai was barren; she had no child. Genesis 11:30

And the Lord appeared unto Abram, and said, Unto thy seed will I give this land: and there builded he an altar unto the Lord, who appeared unto him. Genesis 12:7

Verse 30 seems out of place in this chapter given it did not mention if Nahor's wife was barren. Stating Sarai was barren didn't seem relevant here. However, this was pertinent information to the promise the Lord spoke to Abram in chapter 12 concerning his seed and the land where he was presently dwelling. This scriptural account is a prime example of how God knows the end from the beginning and how sometimes he will share his plans for us with us. He does desire to bless us if we will allow him to guide us to receive his best for us. God's blessings and plans are more than we can imagine. Case in point, God's promise to Abram and Sari.

And the Lord said unto Abram, after that Lot was separated from him, Lift up now thine eyes and look from the place where thou art northward, and southward, and eastward, and westward: Genesis 13:14

For all the land which thou seest, to thee will I give it, and to thy seed forever. Genesis 13:15

And I will make thy seed as the dust of the earth: so that if a man can number the dust of the earth, then shall thy seed also be numbered. Genesis 13:16

This account is considered the Abrahamic Covenant. God promised Abram his seed would be innumerable. Well, the first salutation to Abram from the Lord seemed to speak in a singular tense, however, in Genesis 13:16, this salutation God speaks of Abram's seed as the "dust of the earth". God is so awesome, how he referenced the seed as "dust" and then he says, "then shall thy seed also be numbered". How can one number or count "dust of the earth"? In essence, God was telling Abram, you might be childless (no seed) now, nonetheless, not only will you have a child (seed), you will have an innumerable legacy. Hallelujah!

After these things the word of the Lord came unto Abram in a vision, saying, Fear not, Abram: I am thy shield, and thy exceeding great reward. Genesis 15:1

And Abram said, Lord God, what wilt thou give me, seeing I go childless, and the steward of my house is this Eliezer of Damascus? Genesis 15:2

And Abram said, Behold, to me thou hast given no seed: and, lo, one born in my house is mine heir. Genesis 15:3

And, behold, the word of the Lord came unto him, saying, This shall not be thine heir; but he that come forth out of thine own bowels shall be thine heir. Genesis 15:4

And he brought him forth abroad, and said, Look now toward heaven, and tell the stars, if thou be able to number them: and he said unto him, So shall thy seed be. Genesis 15:5

And he believed in the Lord; and he counted it to him for righteousness. Genesis 15:6

Abram felt the need to mention for the second time to God the problem with his promise. At this point, the promise of the one child hadn't come to pass to even consider his seed being innumerable as the stars. Abram was acknowledging ultimately God was the reason he didn't have a child. He acknowledged

God as his source for every aspect of his life. God let Abram know that he was not limited to the customs of heirship of barren couples, nonetheless, his heir would be of his own bowels (his bloodline or body). As he promised, he and Sarai, his wife, will conceive a child.

Men, I want to evoke the creative ability within you; your semen is life and not a dead substance that expels from your body during sexual intercourse. It is your God-likeness ability to create life, a small person in your image and likeness. This is why casual sex is not ordained by God. Sex is a covenant benefit for married couples. God did not ordain the epidemic we are experiencing from the rebellion of his family order; children out of wedlock and children without the guidance of a father in the home. Fathers are to guide and teach their children about God and life. God's ultimate plan for the "male" man is for him to be a husband and father, not a boyfriend or a baby daddy.

God in his omniscience, Abram's promised seed had a God-given destiny. God had the plan before he gave the child. So, it is with us today, God has a divine plan for every person born in this world. Sometimes when we want something or have an expectation of something, waiting for it to happen can seem forever. This was the case with Sarai, Abram's wife. She decided to help God fulfill his promise to them by suggesting Abram go into her handmaiden Hagar to conceive a child. In this instance, Sarai advised her husband against what God had spoken to him, just as Eve did to Adam. I make mention of this because in our marriage the husband is the head or leader of the family, and the wife needs to be able to acknowledge, as well as, submit to his leadership. I am not saying the husband will have all the answers, of course not, however, God might give him instructions concerning a decision he has asked God for guidance, for this reason, the wife will need to submit to her husband in obedience to God. In acknowledging Abram's failure as the leader of his family, Sarai's suggestion should have been dismissed by Abram based on God's word given to him. God promised him the seed would be of his bowels with his wife and not from any of his servants.

And Hagar bare Abram a son: and Abram called his son's name, which Hagar bare, Ishmael. Genesis 16:15

And when Abram was ninety years old and nine, the Lord appeared to Abram, and said unto him, I am the Almighty God; walk before me, and be thou perfect. Genesis 17:1

And I will make my covenant between me and thee, and will multiply thee exceedingly. Genesis 17:2

And Abram fell on his face: and God talked with him, saying. Genesis 17:3

As for me, behold, my covenant is with thee, and thou shalt be a father of many nations. Genesis 17:4

Neither shall thy name any more be called Abram, but thy name shall be Abraham; for a father of many nations have I made thee. Genesis 17:5

And I will make thee exceeding fruitful, and I will make nations of thee, and kings shall come out of thee. Genesis 17:6

And I will establish my covenant between me and thee and thy seed after thee in their generations for an everlasting covenant, to be a God unto thee, and to thy seed after thee. Genesis 17:7

God reminded Abram he was the Almighty God and for him to be perfect before him, to follow him for the covenant to be fulfilled in his life and the lives of his seed. He reiterated to him the covenant was as he had spoken in times past. The promise was with him and his seed with his wife Sarai. In spite of the fact, he listened to Sarai and had a son with Hagar, it did not change what God had spoken and declared. Ishmael, Hagar's son, could not be the promised child because Hagar was not

Abram's wife. Abraham was not in a marital covenant with Hagar. God declared Sarai as Abraham's wife according to prior scripture texts. For clarity's sake, because Hagar did not qualify to bring forth the promise didn't mean God did not love her. God did love her and cared for her. She was not responsible for the situation she found herself and her son. What God promised had to come to pass as he declared.

And God said unto Abraham, As for Sarai thy wife, thou shalt not call her name Sarai, but Sarah shall her name be. Genesis 17:15

And I will bless her, and give thee a son also of her: Yea, I will bless her, and she shall be a mother of nations; kings of people shall be of her. Genesis 17:16

And God said, Sarah thy wife shall bear thee a son indeed; and thou shalt call his name Isaac: and I will establish my covenant with him for an everlasting covenant, and with his seed after him. Genesis 17:19

And as for Ishmael, I have heard thee: Behold, I have blessed him, and will make him fruitful, and will multiply him exceedingly; twelve princes shall he beget, and I will make him a great nation. Genesis 17:20

But my covenant will I establish with Isaac, which Sarah shall bear unto thee at this set time in the next year. Genesis 17:21

Although Ishmael was not God's choice for the promise, God loved him and had a plan for him. Regardless of the circumstances of conception, God can use anyone for his purpose and glory. In God's eyes, children aren't considered a mistake, especially an unplanned child. The take away regarding Hagar and Ismael not being a part of the Abrahamic covenant, God declared to Abram that the heir would be from his wife, Sari. Hagar was not his wife and going unto her for a seed was totally against God's word, his order and was not in complete faith. Time and challenges in Abraham and Sarah's bodies caused their faith to waiver in the promise of God. We have to remind ourselves God is faithful; when He makes a promise it will come to pass at the appointed time. We have to patiently wait in faith no matter the circumstances.

And the Lord visited Sarah as he had said, and the Lord did unto Sarah as he had spoken. Genesis 21:1

For Sarah conceived, and bare Abraham a son in his old age, at the set time of which God had spoken to him. Genesis 21:2

And Abraham called the name of his son that was born unto him, whom Sarah bare to him, Isaac. Genesis 21:3

It was a total of 25 years Abraham and Sarah waited for their promised son, Isaac. God's promise to Abraham and Sarah was not completely fulfilled after the birth of Isaac. Abraham and Sarah had to continue in faith concerning the promise of an innumerable seed as Isaac grew. Sarah was able to enjoy her blessing for 36 years before she died at the age of 127. She did not live to see the fulfillment of the promise in Isaac's life. After the death of Sarah, Abraham realized Isaac's <u>need</u> for a wife in order for God's promise and plan to be fulfilled. God promised Abraham's seed would be innumerable, at this time, Isaac didn't have a wife to help meet God's plan for his life and the promise to his father Abraham. Abraham charged his servant Eliezer to go seek his son a wife to marry out of Canaan where they dwelled. He instructed his servant to go back to his country and kindred to find Isaac a wife.

And Abraham was old, and well stricken in age: and the Lord had blessed Abraham in all things. Genesis 24:1

And Abraham said unto his eldest servant of his house, that ruled over all that he had, Put, I pray thee, thy hand under my thigh: Genesis 24:2

And I will make thee swear by the Lord, the God of heaven, and the God of the earth, that thou shalt not take a wife unto my son of the daughters of the Canaanites, among whom I dwell: Genesis 24:3

But thou shalt go unto my country, and to my kindred, and take a wife unto my son Isaac. Genesis 24:4

The charge to Abraham's servant was very important. Abraham knew that any woman would not be sufficient for Isaac. Isaac needed a helpmeet. The Canaanites were wicked and idolatrous people. If idols where their gods, a woman from these people would be accustomed to worshipping idols and not the true and living God. Marrying a Canaanite woman that worship idol gods would make Isaac and his wife unequally yoked. She could entice him to stray from following God, which would jeopardize God's promise to Abraham. As believers, we should have a standard concerning our mate. It is wise to consider the religious belief of your prospective mate. Remember, they are to be a helpmeet, assist in seeking and fulfilling the will of God for your life and your lives together as a married couple.

Abraham's servant, Eliezer, knew the weight of his master's charge to him concerning finding his son Isaac a wife. I believe Abraham's faithful walk before God was observed by Eliezer, so Eliezer decides to pray and ask God for his divine help in discerning the right wife for Isaac.

And he said, O Lord God of my master Abraham, I pray thee, send me good speed this day, and shew kindness unto my master Abraham. Genesis 24:12

Behold, I stand here by the well of water; and the daughters of the men of the city come out to draw water: Genesis 24:13

And let it come to pass, that the damsel to whom I shall say, Let down thy pitcher, I pray thee, that I may drink; and she shall say, Drink, and I will give thy camels drink also; let the same be she that thou hast appointed for thy servant Isaac; and thereby shall I know that thou hast shewed kindness unto my master. Genesis 24:14

And it came to pass, before he had done speaking, that, behold, Rebekah came out, who was born to Bethuel, son of Milcah, the wife of Nahor, Abraham's brother, with her pitcher upon her shoulder. Genesis 24:15

And the damsel was very fair to look upon, a virgin, neither had any man known her: and she went down to the well, and filled her pitcher, and came up. Genesis 24:16

And the servant ran to meet her, and said, Let me, I pray thee, drink a little water of thy pitcher. Genesis 24:17

And she said, Drink, my lord: and she hasted, and let down her pitcher upon her hand, and gave him drink. Genesis 24:18

And when she had done giving him drink, she said, I will draw water for thy camels also, until they have done drinking. Genesis 24:19

And she hasted, and emptied her pitcher into the trough, and ran again unto the well to draw water, and drew for all his camels. Genesis 24:20

God answered Eliezer's pray request concerning the sign that would signify God's choice for Isaac's wife. Some people believe God is not concern about the person we choose to marry. They believe God gives us free will, so, it is our choice to choose who we desire to marry. If one believes this way, so be it, however, this scriptural account of Rebekah being chosen to be Isaac's wife proves God will assist you in choosing a spouse if you so desire his help. God knows the heart of a person and he knows your future, welcoming him in all aspects of your life is prudent and wise.

Eliezer's prayer request would, in essence, reveal the character of the woman. Rebekah's response to Eliezer revealed her character, she was kind and thoughtful. Character is the sum of a person, not the outer appearance. Selflessness, kindness, and hospitality are a few qualities a wife should possess to be a suitable helper. A wife must be willing to help her husband in his endeavors in life and vice versa. She should be an asset to help him build a legacy and wealth for their family.

In verse 16, God saw fit to mention Rebekah's virginity. It is not recorded in this scripture text that Eliezer prayed for the damsel to be a virgin to fulfill the virginity custom. However, God established the laws and customs, so he had to honor his word for Isaac's prospective wife.

And Isaac came from the way of the well Lahairoi; for he dwelt in the south country. Genesis 24:62

And Isaac went out to meditate in the field at the eventide: and he lifted up his eyes, and saw, and, behold, the camels were coming. Genesis 24:63

And Rebekah lifted up her eyes, and when she saw Isaac, she lighted off the camel. Genesis 24:64

For she had said unto the servant, What man is this that walketh in the field to meet us? And the servant had said, It is my master: therefore, she took a veil, and covered herself. Genesis 24:65

And the servant told Isaac all things that he had done. Genesis 24:66

And Isaac brought her into his mother Sarah's tent, and took Rebekah, and she became his wife; and he loved her; and Isaac was comforted after his mother's death. Genesis 24:67

Think about this, Rebekah left her family to travel to a strange land with a stranger to be a wife to someone she never met. Can you imagine agreeing to marry someone you never meet? I believe she agreed to go with Eliezer because of Eliezer's testimony. She wanted to honor God's choice for her to be Isaac's wife. The scripture text does not speak of Isaac and Rebekah had a feast or vow ceremony to signify their marital covenant, however, the scriptures tell us Isaac took Rebekah into his deceased mother's tent and she became his wife and he was comforted. Rebekah became Isaac's wife by God's choice and consummation or the act of sexual intercourse. The sex act is an act of becoming in covenant with the other person. Giving yourself sexually to another person other than your spouse, you are, in essence, breaking your "vow" of the covenant with your spouse and God. It is not a casual act as the world would like to believe. We are so conditioned to do whatever gives us pleasure and ignore what we know God has established in his word. In God's mind, sex is an act of covenant.

As we read the details of Isaac and Rebekah's union, we can agree it is unorthodox for today's society. Today, there's a gradual advancement in the relationship before "love" is expressed or declared in most cases. Surprisingly, in verse 67, the text said, "… and he loved her". Was it "love at first sight" or "purpose"? Isaac didn't know Rebekah prior to her being presented to him. They didn't have a long courtship or engagement. Would it be safe to conclude it was "purpose"? Isaac learned to trust the leading of the Lord from his father and he knew God had a purpose and a plan for his life. So, knowing God's plan for his life and understanding his need for a wife, Isaac readily "loved" Rebekah. Both Isaac and Rebekah understood the significance of God's institution of marriage and the family lineage. Unfortunately, today's culture does not reverence God to this degree to submit to his will, nor understand the importance of the family lineage and heritage, spiritually and naturally.

In Genesis 24:65, the text states, "when Rebekah came near to Isaac, she covered herself with a veil". This account is profound, the veil symbolizes modesty and purity. The veil is worn as a symbol of purity to the husbandman, in which, he unveils his bride to consummate their union. Rebekah was signifying her purity in covering herself before Isaac. Isaac didn't get to "try the milk before he bought the cow". It is believed sex should be experienced before the wedding to ensure compatibility after the marriage. We know this ideology is immature and goes against God's order. To govern oneself to God's standard requires an individual to truly love God and maturity. I don't believe Isaac's love for Rebekah was based on her ability to satisfy him sexually. He believed Rebekah was God's choice for him and that was the most important component in his love for Rebekah. He chose to honor God and his purpose for their lives together.

Each spouse in the marriage has to love God first and far most to stay in the marriage till death do you part. Many marriages end in divorce, not solely because of the lack of feelings for their spouse, it is because the love for God was not strong enough to submit to God's way. The refusal to sacrificially Love (to **die** to self) causes division in the marriage and divorce is inevitable. To love is to die! Each spouse must choose to humble themselves and honor their "vow" to God and their spouse to save the marriage. The marriage "vow" is first actually to God. You are promising yourself to the other individual to love and take care of them as God has outlined in his word. This is why selfishness will kill a marriage. If each party is selfless, they both will consider the needs and wants of their spouse. Neither one will be depleted in the marriage as is often the case in a divorce. Before becoming involved with someone, it's imperative for both persons to have a true relationship with God and desire to honor him with their life.

As we continue to look at the story of Isaac and Rebekah, we find the same pathology with them as Isaac's father and mother. God's promise was once again challenged by barrenness.

And Isaac intreated the Lord for his wife because she was barren: and the Lord was intreated of him, and Rebekah his wife conceived. Genesis 25:21

And the children struggled together within her; and she said, If it be so, why am I thus? And she went to enquire of the Lord. Genesis 25:22

I believe Isaac sought the Lord for Rebekah because he knew God's promise to his father, Abraham. He knew that he needed a seed to fulfill the promise. Isaac knew God promised, so ultimately, he was their source of deliverance. He learned how to worship and relate to God from his father. Also, when Eliezer and Rebekah came back from their journey to Isaac, the scripture text stated Isaac had been in meditation in the field.

Genesis 25:21 is a good example to women the importance of having a Godly husband, a man that know God, know the power of God, know the power of prayer, as well as lives by God's word. In difficult times, your husband will know the source of deliverance for you and his household. So, in the challenge of Rebekah's barrenness, Isaac petitioned God for Rebekah and the Lord answered his prayer for her to conceive.

In verse 22 of Genesis 25, Rebekah prayed to the Lord for insight on what was going on in her body with the twins she had conceived. She knew something was strange about her pregnancy, so she inquired of the Lord for insight. Isaac and Rebekah both believed in God and understood God was their source for every aspect of their life. They were not influenced by the idol gods served by the Canaanites in the land. They served the one and only living God. Being equally yoked in belief and being on one accord in the relationship are key components.

And the Lord said unto her, Two nations are in thy womb, and two manner of people shall be separated from thy bowels: and the one people shall be stronger than the other people: and the elder shall serve the younger. Genesis 25:23

And when her days to be delivered were fulfilled, behold, there were twins in her womb. Genesis 25:24

And the first came out red, all over like an hairy garment; and they called his name Esau. Genesis 25:25

And after that came his brother out, and his hand took hold on Esau's heel; and his name was called Jacob: and Isaac was threescore years old when she bare them. Genesis 25:26

When you read these scriptures, you might think these accounts are not for the generations of today. Let me remind you as I stated before, within the male and female body is creative ability. The seeds within you (the male being) are not just mere sperm cells. In the first part of verse 23, "and the Lord said unto her, Two nations are in thy womb...". We must renew our minds to God's purpose for creating Adam and Eve and even ourselves. His purpose still stands today. We are kingdom people with a kingdom building agenda. We are charged to be fruitful and multiply God's kingdom by producing natural and spiritual offspring. Spiritually, as we live by his standards and not our own or the world's, we are building his kingdom on earth by influencing others with our lifestyle.

I BESEECH you therefore, brethren, by the mercies of God, that ye present your bodies a living sacrifice, holy, acceptable unto God, which is your reasonable service. Romans 12:1

And be not conformed to this world: but be ye transformed by the renewing of your mind, that ye may prove what is that good, and acceptable, and perfect will of God. Romans 12:2

In today's society, God's plan for the natural marital union is not the standard any longer. The following relationships are prevalent today:

-friends with benefits relationships/situationships

-sugar daddy/sugar mama relationships

-co-habitation/shacking relationships

-Common-law marriage

-lesbian/homosexual relationships

-side chick/side piece relationships

All of these relationships are illegal sexually-based relationships and are against God's design and purpose for his creation. Holy Matrimony is God's desire; however, marriage is no longer the goal for many. One of the greatest attacks Satan has devised to pervert God's design for the marital union is the lust for same-sex relationships. Let me be clear in what I am conveying, the same-sex relationship is not a greater sin than a heterosexual illegal sexual relationship. God's word has the only authority to define God's mind concerning the marital covenant and union. God's purpose for the natural marital union can never be fulfilled in a same-sex relationship. The scripture clearly says, "God blessed them and God said unto them, "Be fruitful and multiply and replenish the earth." The scripture also says, "…and the Lord God said, It is not good that the man should be alone; I will make him a helpmeet for him." The text is not talking about Adam's need for a sex partner. Adam's need was for a suitable helper, a human being that could receive his seed and produce life (a seed) after their likeness. A helper to help him meet God's charge to be fruitful, multiply and replenish the earth. Same-sex relationships can never create life as God designed and purposed, male and female.

A helpmeet is a counterpart/opposite match. I read a commentary defining help meet in scripture on the internet. [Tuesday, November 9, 2010 www.womeninthescriptures.com]

The Real Meaning of the Term "Help MEET".

It stated that the Hebrew word "ezer" means help or salvation. The commentary went on to say that Eve was not only created to be his helper or his companion, rather she was to be his savior and deliverer. I know this sounds off target, but I understood what the writer was trying to convey. The writer went on to say, "Women are a savior to men by the fact that they give them life and nurture them towards the light of Christ. For it was through a woman, Mary, that Jesus Christ came to conquer the bonds of death and sin and atoned Adam's transgression. Without a woman to bear the body of Christ, mankind would have been lost and fallen forever. Adam's work and purpose on the earth would have been meaningless. Mary was the gateway that made Christ's work possible and her nurturing the catalyst for his success. Even though Eve, didn't give physical life to Adam, she saved him from spiritual death by opening the way for the Savior and Redeemer to come into the world. Salvation in the form of Christ literally came to the earth through a woman.

Realistically, there are married couples that are barren as Sara/Abraham and Rebekah/Isaac were at one time. They were unable to reproduce life, not because of improper compatibility, rather, physical issues until God's appointed time. The reality of couples that may be challenged with barrenness doesn't negate a couple's ability to build God's family unit. Couples can seek God on being foster parents, adopting a child or children, or maybe being surrogate parents to children within their extended families. Giving yourselves to love and teaching children about life and God in your sphere of influence as you would your own child.

Being fruitful and multiplying not only applies to the natural union, but it also applies to the spiritual union with God. We, as believers are to be united as one with God through our obedience and alignment with his word. As we live our lives; we are to be examples of the glorious life in him on the earth to draw people to him to increase his kingdom.

Ye are the salt of the earth: but if the salt have lost his savour, wherewith shall it be salted? It is thenceforth good for nothing, but to be cast out, and to be trodden under foot of men. St. Matthew 5:13

Ye are the light of the world. A city that is set on an hill cannot be hid. St. Matthew 5:14

Neither do men light a candle, and put it under a bushel, but on a candlestick; and it giveth light unto all that are in the house. St. Matthew 5:15

Let your light so shine before men, that they may see your good works, and glorify your Father which is in heaven. St. Matthew 5:16

Single or married, we are charged to live to build God's kingdom. Spiritually, we are to live our lives so others will see a difference in our way of life from the world. Compelling them to see their need for a God-centered life and fellowship with God. To multiply God's family, he has placed gifts and callings in each of us. We have to seek him concerning the gift(s) and how to utilize them effectively and for his glory. As a couple, you may be called to be pastors, youth leaders, worship leaders or start a non-profit mentoring youth, or teach Sunday school at your local church. Not all gifts are spiritual gifts, you might have a passion to be a teacher, lawyer, doctor, counselor, motivational speaker, help underprivileged people or a helper in any capacity. We are all to be fruitful in being a witness and example of our Lord and Savior. Building the kingdom of God on earth is the objective of our life, our reason for being.

And Jesus went about all the cities and villages, teaching in their synagogues, and preaching the gospel of the kingdom, and healing every sickness and every disease among the people. St. Matthew 9:35

But when he saw the multitudes, he was moved with compassion on them, because they fainted, and were scattered abroad, as sheep having no shepherd. St. Matthew 9:36

Then saith he unto his disciples, The harvest truly is plenteous, but the labourers are few; St. Matthew 9:37

Pray ye therefore the Lord of the harvest, that he will send forth labourers into his harvest. St. Matthew 9:38

CHAPTER SEVEN:
"Before you say "Yes", and I "Do"

Singleness

In singleness, you are to become one with God after repentance and accepting Jesus Christ as your Lord and Savior. This is a representation of the spiritual union (covenant) with God. God's desire to have an intimate love relationship with you as he and Adam had in the garden. Obedience is the expression of "Love" to God. It's what makes him smile? He wants you to himself before he brings a mate in your life, as he did with Adam before he created Eve. When you have fallen in love with God, as well as, commit and submit your life to God in your singleness, it is during this time you are becoming whole within yourself. You are able to take the time necessary to seek God to discover the gifts and passion he has placed in you. The ability to serve God with your whole heart and work out your own soul salvation is best developed in your singleness. You can seek him without distraction from obligations to another intimate relationship in your life. You are soberly able to evaluate issues in your life that may need to be addressed and resolved before getting into a relationship with someone. Take this time to develop self- LOVE, self-esteem, and discipline. Be the person you would want to marry. Whatever standards you require in a mate, you meet your own standards first.

Make God your husband for he cares deeply about you and the destiny he has for you. Live spiritually pure to God so he can trust you to remain pure in a courtship or relationship.

For thy Maker is thine husband; the Lord of host is his name; and thy Redeemer the Holy One of Israel; The God of the whole earth shall he be called. Isaiah 54:5

Union

Before joining with another person, make God your husband, unite spiritually with God. Becoming one with God, allows his spirit to dwell in you and allows you to discover who you are in Christ. So, when your counterpart is revealed, you both will be ready and equipped to make this beautiful lifetime commitment. Being one with God is the foundation of a good healthy holy union. You will understand submission because you will have learned to submit yourself to God. Considering God's thoughts on decisions you desire to make before you make them. You will understand how to relinquish the mindset of "I" to "us". In your natural union, your mindset has to change from "I" to "us". Marriage is two people giving selflessly 100% for the health and success of the relationship. Two individuals with different likes and dislikes, therefore, communication is essential to be successful in the marriage. So, have a set time in your day to talk to each other without distractions. Taking this time will build a deeper level of intimacy in your relationship. Also, take the time to learn your mate's LOVE language; what says, "I Love You" to your mate? Is it **"acts of kindness", "words of affirmation", "gifts", "quality time"** or maybe **"physical touch"?** Learning their love language will keep their love tank full and no opportunity for the enemy of your marriage.

Let the husband render unto the wife due benevolence: and likewise also the wife unto the husband. 1 Corinthians 7:3

The wife hath no power of her own body, but the husband: and likewise also the husband hath not power of his own body, but the wife. I Corinthians 7:4

Defraud ye not one the other, except it be with consent for a time, that ye may give yourselves to fasting and prayer; and come together again, that Satan tempt you not for your incontinency. I Corinthians 7:5

But I speak this by permission, and not of commandment. I Corinthians 7:6

May I remind you; sex was created by God for married couples as a covenant benefit. Yes, sex is the method to procreate, however, God made it pleasurable to be enjoyed as often as a couple desires. So, be sure to render to your spouse due sexual intimacy; do not become fraudulent in your marriage. Withholding sex from your spouse as a weapon, form of manipulation and control is wrong and ungodly behavior. Your body is not your own in a marital covenant. No, I am not saying you are to allow your spouse to abuse you in any way. I am saying your spouse has sexual needs you should meet within reason in your marital covenant. Sidenote, sexual appetite and styles need to be discussed and agreed upon before "I Do". If you truly love your spouse, it is your desire to meet their sexual need, as well as, being welling to abstain briefly for fasting or physical ailment.

Comparative to the natural union, the spiritual union with God, we are one with him in the spirit. Our body the dwelling place for the Holy Spirit after repentance and salvation. We are no longer "lord" (self- governing) of our life. It's no more "I" but "God" that governs our life through his word. Through obedience to his word and consecrated prayer time we develop an intimate relationship with him.

But he that is joined unto the Lord is one spirit. 1 Corinthians 6:17

What? Know ye not that your body is the temple of the Holy Ghost which is in you, which ye have of God, and ye are not your own? 1 Corinthians 6:19

For ye are bought with a price: therefore, glorify God in your body, and in your spirit, which are God's. 1 Corinthians 6:20

Allowing God to be the center of your love and your union, your marriage is destined to be full of blessings and withstand the test of time. Marriage is a gift, enjoy it to the fullest. Your union will be a three-cord union not easily broken.

And if one prevail against him, two shall withstand him; and a threefold cord is not quickly broken. Ecclesiastes 4:12

'Til Death Do You Part

In hope of eternal life, which God, that cannot lie, promised before the world began; Titus 1:2

But after that the kindness and love of God our Saviour toward man appeared, Titus 3:4

Not by works of righteousness which we have done, but according to his mercy he saved us, by the washing of regeneration, and renewing of the Holy Ghost; Titus 3:5

Which he shed on us abundantly through Jesus Christ our Saviour; Titus 3:6

That being justified by his grace, we should be made heirs according to the hope of eternal life. Titus 3:7

As God planned from the beginning, the union of the male and female to carry out his KINGDOM PURPOSE on the earth was designed for a lifetime. Adam and Eve had a perfect existence in the garden and in the presence of God. Adam's sin caused the separation from God and the penalty of "death" upon mankind. Our union with our spouse is " 'til death do you part"; meaning, only by the physical death of a spouse, separation takes place in the union. Realistically, today, separation and dissolutions of marriages are happening for all kinds of reasons. Selfishness is usually the main culprit, whether it exhibits itself through an adulterous relationship, abusive behavior, or falling out of love with a spouse. This is why it is imperative that both parties are to be healthy, whole, and filled with God's spirit. You have to be delivered from selfishness and learn to be selfless for the success of the marriage. Christ was selfless and he perfectly did the will of God. Sacrificing his life to reconcile us back to God with the promise of eternal life with him. He is our example on how to live unto God and carry out his purpose and will for our life. Keep in mind, the natural marriage covenant is symbolic of the spiritual union with God, the Creator, and his creation, the human being. In the natural union, a separation was only to come by death. So, it is with our spiritual relationship with God, after being reconciled to him our relationship with him is supposed to be a never-ending relationship as well. When Adam sinned, it did not change God's plan to have a never-ending relationship with us, it changed the dynamics of the relationship. God is "holy" and Adam's sin caused him and all generations after him to be "unholy". God in his omniscient, He implemented a plan to reconcile us back to himself through the death and resurrection of his Son, Jesus Christ. If we confess Jesus Christ as God's Son and accept him in our life as our Lord and Savior, we are reconciled to God. Free to obey God's word and relate to him personally.

The death, burial, and resurrection of Christ is the gift of salvation, reconciliation, and eternal peace to us. Christ came to do the will of God for mankind. He knew his purpose and he knew he could not be contaminated by the world system. Christ glorified his Father in everything he did because he knew his assignment and its importance. He loved his Father and all the generations of the world so much; he offered himself as a sacrifice for the plan of redemption and reconciliation. In obedience to the will of God, Christ died on the cross for us. The omnipotent God raised Jesus from death to life in heaven with Him for eternity. This is the blessed hope we have in the crucifixion of Christ. Crucifying our fleshy desires and receiving the indwelling of the spirit of God, when our life on earth is complete, God promises to raise us from death to life in eternity with Him. The natural death is the gateway to entering into the eternal presence of God. Hallelujah! Hallelujah! Glory to the Lamb of God!

For when we were yet without strength, in due time Christ died for the ungodly. Romans 5:6

For scarcely for a righteous man will one die: yet peradventure for a good man some would even dare to die. Romans 5:7

But God commendeth his love toward us, in that, while we were yet sinners, Christ died for us. Romans 5:8

Much more then, being now justified by his blood, we shall be saved from wrath through him. Romans 5:9

For if, when we were enemies, were reconciled to God by the death of his Son, much more, being reconciled, we shall be saved by his life. Romans 5:10

By this we know that we love the children of God, when we love God, and keep his commandments. I John 5:2

For this is the love of God, that we keep his commandments: and his commandments are not grievous. I John 5:3

For whatsoever is born of God overcometh the world: and this is the victory that overcometh the world, even our faith. I John 5:4

He that believeth on the Son of God hath the witness in himself: he that believeth not God hath made him a liar; because he believeth not the record that God gave of his Son. I John 5:10

Prayer of Encouragement

Father God, I thank you for the person that has availed themselves to reading this book. To understand your word on the spiritual and natural covenant. I pray that through this book they have been enlightened to a new or renewed relationship with you, the lover of their soul. Father, I pray they understand and receive your love for them and who you have created them to be. It is because of your love for mankind that you sent your only begotten Son to redeem us. Through his sacrificial death, we are made righteous and are reconciled to you. We are able to have a personal relationship with you our Heavenly Father. I thank you for this blessed hope in spending eternity in your presence.

Lord, I pray that you will reveal yourself in a greater way, that you will be glorified in their life. Whether they are single or married at this time, Lord I pray they will seek you First in every aspect of their life because you care for them and you have a purpose for their existence on the earth.

In Jesus' Name I pray. Amen

Prayer of Salvation

Father, I know I was born with a sinful nature and I am in need of your salvation through the blood of your only begotten Son, Jesus the Christ. Forgive me of every sin I sinned against you and I ask you to create in me a clean heart and renew the right spirit within me. Father, deliver me from every generational curse that may have taken preeminence in my family lineage. Fill me with your Holy Spirit to lead me and guide me as I commit my life to your will and way. Help me to be the person you have ordained me to be for your glory. Father, I thank you for your forgiveness and for accepting me as your child. In Jesus' name. Amen

1John 1:9

If we confess our sins, he is faithful and just to forgive us our sins, and to cleanse us from all unrighteousness.

Romans 10:9-10

That if you confess with your mouth the Lord Jesus, and shalt believe in your heart that God has raised Him from the dead, you will be saved. For with the heart one believeth unto righteousness, and with the mouth confession is made unto salvation.

Revelation 19:7-9

Let us be glad and rejoice, and give honour to him: for the marriage of the Lamb is come, and his wife hath made herself ready. And to her was granted that she should be arrayed in fine linen, clean and white: for the fine linen is the righteousness of saints. And he saith unto me, Write, Blessed are they which are called unto the marriage supper of the Lamb. And he saith unto me, These are the true sayings of God.

Be fruitful and multiply God's kingdom by
producing godly natural and spiritual offspring

Resources

1. Scripture is taken from the DAKE'S ANNOTATED REFERENCE BIBLE. The Old and New Testaments, with Notes, Concordance, and Index, Copyright 1063, 1991

2. Webster New Dictionary of the English Language New Edition Webster's Revised Unabridged

3. Merriam-Webster.com Wikepedia.com Biblestudytools.com

4. Biblestudytools.com - Easton Bible Dictionary

5. www.gotquestions.com

6. Oxforddictionaries.com www.womeninthescriptures.com www.dictionary.com

7. Five Love Languages: The Secret to Love that Lasts by Gary Chapman

8. Book cover design by Jamacia Johnson - Amplicreative.com

www.ingramcontent.com/pod-product-compliance
Lightning Source LLC
LaVergne TN
LVHW051501070426
835507LV00022B/2877